Attitudes toward Economic Inequality

Attitudes toward Economic Inequality

Everett Carll Ladd
and Karlyn H. Bowman

THE AEI PRESS

Publisher for the American Enterprise Institute
WASHINGTON, D.C.

1998

Available in the United States from the AEI Press, c/o
Publisher Resources Inc., 1224 Heil Quaker Blvd., P.O.
Box 7001, La Vergne, TN 37086-7001. Call toll-free 1-
800-269-6267. Distributed outside the U.S. by arrange-
ment with Eurospan, 3 Henrietta Street, London WC2E
8LU England.

ISBN 0-8447-7090-6

1 3 5 7 9 10 8 6 4 2

THE AEI PRESS
Publisher for the American Enterprise Institute
1150 Seventeenth Street, N.W.
Washington, D.C. 20036

Printed in the United States of America

Contents

Foreword

This study is one of a series commissioned by the American Enterprise Institute on trends in the level and distribution of U.S. wages, income, wealth, consumption, and other measures of material welfare. The issues addressed in the series involve much more than dry statistics: they touch on fundamental aspirations of the American people—material progress, widely shared prosperity, and just reward for individual effort—and affect popular understanding of the successes and shortcomings of the private market economy and of particular government policies. For these reasons, discussions of "economic inequality" in the media and political debate are often partial and partisan as well as superficial. The AEI series is intended to improve the public discussion by bringing new data to light, exploring the strengths and weaknesses of various measures of economic welfare, and highlighting important questions of interpretation, causation, and consequence.

Each study in the series is presented and discussed in draft form at an AEI seminar prior to publication by the AEI Press. Marvin Kosters, director of economic policy studies at AEI, organized the series and moderated the seminars. A current list of published studies appears on the last page.

CHRISTOPHER DEMUTH
President, American Enterprise Institute

Acknowledgments

We would like to thank a number of individuals who helped us with this monograph. Lisa Ferraro Parmelee of the Roper Center at the University of Connecticut read the manuscript and offered many constructive stylistic and editorial comments. Rob Persons, also of the Roper Center, scoured the data archive for relevant questions. Melissa Knauer at AEI proofed many drafts of the manuscript and did the time-consuming task of constructing the tables and checking them for accuracy. AEI editor Ann Petty used her excellent editing skills to move readers through significant amounts of data. Three interns—Peter Baker, Sarah Owen, and Nathan Gragg—searched for data and checked facts. We are grateful for their assistance.

1

Introduction

A cover story in the *Economist* a few years ago reported that "income inequalities in America and Britain are greater than at any time in the past 50 years." The magazine suggested that concerns about the issue "played a big role in Bill Clinton's election victory in 1992, and are likely to loom large in Britain's general election."[1] Many in the United States appeared to agree on the political importance of the issue. Treasury Secretary Robert Rubin, Democrat Bill Bradley, and Republican Jack Kemp were among the prominent politicians, economists, and pollsters who participated in a 1995 forum on the subject. The *Washington Post* summarized the discussion this way: "The growing income gap between rich and the poor has become the central issue in American politics, and the party that figures out what to do about it—or that makes the right noises about it—will dominate American politics."[2]

In early 1996, the issue seemed to gain momentum. "Corporate Killers," a *Newsweek* cover story, included

---

In a round-table discussion at AEI on November 21, 1996, Stanley Greenberg of Greenberg-Quinlan Research, Inc., and Guy Molyneux of Peter D. Hart Research Associates commented on arguments made in an early version of this paper. Greenberg pictures of nine CEOs, their salaries, and the number of workers their corporations had laid off.[3] Republican presidential candidate Patrick Buchanan talked about "corporate butchers," and Robert Dole, the eventual Republican nominee, argued that "corporate profits are setting records and so are corporate layoffs. . . . The bond market finished a spectacular year. But the real average hourly wage is 5 percent lower than it was a decade ago."[4]

During his tenure as labor secretary to President Clinton, Robert Reich warned about the "anxious class" and the "dangerous shift in the distribution of income away from ordinary working Americans to the very wealthy who own most of America's financial assets."[5] On leaving his post in early 1997, he spoke about the unfinished agenda of addressing inequality, which Reich described as "greater than at any time in living memory."[6] After the words "greater than at any time in living memory." In a speech to the Kennedy School of Government in December 1997, Democratic House Minority Leader Richard Gephardt echoed these themes.

As we complete this monograph, a steady stream of positive economic news has pushed coverage of inequality from the front pages, but concerns about what is happening and why continue to preoccupy economists

is a prominent Democratic pollster and author of *Middle-Class Dreams: The Politics and Power of the New American Majority.* His article, "Private Heroism and Public Purpose" (*American Prospect,* September– October 1996), continues his exploration of themes in the book and addresses issues of inequality and fairness. Molyneux, a vice-president of Peter D. Hart Research Associates, has been involved in many Democratic campaigns. He is the coauthor, with Ethel Klein, of *Corporate Irresponsibility: There Ought to Be Some Laws* (Washington, D.C.: Preamble Center for Public Policy, July 1996), a study of political and policy implications of attitudes toward corporate America. We are grateful for their comments and have tried to address the points they raised.

and policy makers. Here we offer no opinions about whether or why the income gap is widening. Instead, we use polls to look at public understanding of issues that touch on economic inequality. We also explore what the polls can tell us about whether issues that *relate to* inequality are more salient politically than in the past.

We use the words *relate to* for good reason. Pollsters appear to have concluded, correctly in our view, that buzzwords such as *economic inequality*—common in policy discussions—do not convey much to most Americans. Thus, only a few survey questions actually use these words. Surveyors have instead explored underlying attitudes that bear on how issues of equality and inequality are seen. The purpose of this monograph is to explore these core attitudes. We begin by summarizing the relevant data on attitudes toward wealth and poverty: there is some ambivalence about wealth in the United States but no particular resentment. We turn next to the reasons for this lack of resentment.

Americans tolerate great differences in wealth if they believe that opportunity is broadly present. Therefore, it is particularly important to examine what people say about opportunity. Do people think that it is present for most Americans? For themselves? Have such judgments changed over time? What are the expectations for the next generation? For people's own children? These are, perhaps, the most important questions to answer in this investigation, but they are also the most difficult. Only a handful of survey trends exists for any of these questions.

Equality of opportunity is a demanding social standard. It requires that people perceive the rules of the game to be fair. If they believe that this is the case, they put up with disparities in income and status. If people believe that the rules are being rigged to favor one group or another, inequality could become a more important political issue. Beyond this, society requires that certain standards of behavior be observed up and down the social and economic ladders. High salaries for CEOs, entertainers, or the media are not seen as inherently unjust. But, at some point, they may be seen as unseemly or excessive, upsetting the social equilibrium. Flaunting wealth or status is offensive, and this too could fuel resentment.

Last, we look at what people want the government to do about the differences between the rich and the poor. Do they want the government to limit wealth? To redistribute income from those at the top to those at the middle or the bottom? The answers to these questions provide some clues about whether public concerns about inequality are intensifying.

Data from abroad are available on some of the dimensions discussed above, and we have included them in the appendix. Polls in the areas we are examining reveal some striking cross-national differences. They reinforce the view that America continues to differ from other industrial democracies in its approach to issues concerning inequality—as it does on other ideological dimensions.

2

Opinions about Wealth

What Constitutes Wealth

In 1987, Roper Starch Worldwide began asking a series of questions about income needs. The survey firm asked people how much they and their families would need just to get by, to live in reasonable comfort, and to fulfill all their dreams. Roper has repeated the questions a handful of times since. In 1987, the median response to the question about what was needed to get by was a modest $20,000. To live in reasonable comfort? The median response was $30,000. In 1987, to fulfill all your dreams would have required $50,000 a year. This series of questions was updated in July 1996 by the Roper Center for Public Opinion Research at the University of Connecticut in a survey for *Reader's Digest*. The median amount needed just to get by was $30,000. People thought that they and their families would need $40,000 to live in reasonable comfort, a figure that is close to the figure for median family income today. The median response for the amount needed to fulfill all your dreams was $90,000 (table 2–1).

When Gallup asked in 1990 what "constitutes being rich in America today," the median response of $95,000 was close to the responses given to the question above about fulfilling dreams. Not surprisingly,

5

there were significant differences in responses by income level. A majority (52 percent) of those making under $20,000 a year put the threshold at $100,000; only 11 percent of those earning $100,000 did. The median response was $100,000 when the organization rephrased the question in 1996 to ask how much money per year the respondent would need to consider himself rich.

In its exploration of attitudes about wealth, Gallup probed the respondents' desire to be rich and how likely they thought that was. In Gallup surveys in 1990 and 1996, roughly four in ten said that they did not want to be rich, but six in ten said that they would like to be (table 2–2). The Gallup responses showed interesting differences among groups. In both years, men were more likely than women to want to become rich (65 to 55 percent in 1996). In both surveys, those with higher levels of formal education and income expressed more interest in wealth than those with lower levels. In 1996, 70 percent of college graduates, compared with only 43 percent of those who had not finished high school, wanted to be rich. Seventy-one percent of those earning $75,000 a year expressed a desire to be rich, compared with 47 percent of those making less than $15,000. And, finally, being rich was an aspiration for the young far more than for the old.

On the likelihood of becoming wealthy, the 1990 and 1996 Gallup results are remarkably similar. About 10 percent in both years said this was very likely, and slightly under a quarter called it somewhat likely. The number answering not very likely was 32 percent in 1990 and 37 percent in 1996. And the "not at all likely" response was 35 percent in 1990, and 27 percent in 1996. On this question once again, there were significant differences by age, with young people expressing the greatest optimism about this possibility. Slightly over 60 percent of eighteen- to twenty-nine-year-olds saw at least some likelihood of becoming rich, compared with only 13 percent of those fifty and older (table 2–2). A more recent Princeton Survey Research Associates survey for *Newsweek* provides similar results to the Gallup ones.

Ambivalence, Not Resentment

Given people's modest expectations of what it would take for them to be rich, we might expect resentment of those who have amassed great fortunes, but surveys do not suggest this is the case. The rich are not, however, universally admired, and Americans think that society now places too much emphasis on money. But general attitudes are certainly not hostile, not even particularly unfriendly.

In an Elmo Roper poll conducted for *Fortune* in 1942, high school students were asked whether the country would be better or worse off without rich people. A huge majority of students said that the country would be worse off. In a 1979 Roper Starch Worldwide national survey, 24 percent said that the country would be better off without millionaires, but 51 percent thought that it would be worse off. When the question was repeated in 1992, roughly the same number (21 percent) responded that the country would do better without millionaires, while 44 percent disagreed. Thirty-four percent, had no opinion (table 2–3).

Twice in the 1970s—but, unfortunately, not again— Roper Starch Worldwide asked whether people were against different things. In both years, fewer than 10 percent claimed to be antirich. In 1979, roughly four times that many called themselves antihippy (35 percent), antismoking (28 percent), and antiwelfare (27 percent).

In 1990, a majority, 55 percent, told Gallup that the United States had about the right number of rich people, 21 percent said that the country had too many, and almost as many, 15 percent, answered that the country had too few (table 2–4). In the same survey, over six in ten of those who said they were not rich (almost everyone in the sample) agreed that America benefits from having a class of rich people (table 2–5).

A lack of resentment does not imply approbation. In the 1990 Gallup survey, for example, 52 percent said they admired and respected rich people, but a significant 41 percent said that they did not. In 1992, 45 percent told Roper Starch Worldwide that the wealthy had too much power and influence over the country's policies; about the same percentage felt that way about the press (41 percent). Large business corporations were named by 35 percent, and government departments and bureaus, by 30 percent. In each iteration of this question, the rich were at or near the top as having too much power and influence over how the country was run (table 2–6).

A battery of questions asked about millionaires by Roper Starch Worldwide in 1979 and again in 1992 underscores our mixed views. Sixty-seven percent in 1992 said that millionaires used their wealth to protect their own positions in society. According to 61 percent, they do not pay their fair share of taxes; this finding is familiar to those who review poll data. A majority (55 percent) generally agreed that millionaires' investments created jobs and helped provide prosperity, and 54 percent said their spending provided employment to a lot of people. People were divided about whether millionaires got where they were by exploiting others. Relevant to this inquiry was the statement that millionaires "keep the common man from having his proper share of the wealth." Three in ten thought this was generally true of millionaires (table 2–7).

Only six of these responses changed by five percentage points or more between 1979 and 1992. In 1979, 66 percent agreed that millionaires did not pay their fair share of taxes (61 percent in 1992); 68 percent, that millionaires' investments created jobs and helped provide prosperity (55 percent in 1992); 63 percent (54 percent in 1992), that millionaires' spending employed many people; 58 percent (50 percent in 1992), that millionaires contributed generously to charitable causes; 41 percent (46 percent in 1992), that the wealthy worked hard to earn what they had; and 50 percent (45 percent in 1992), that millionaires made illegal campaign contributions.

In July 1997, Princeton Survey Research Associates did a survey to accompany a *Newsweek* story on the new rich. People were asked their impressions of the new generation of wealthy people and previous generations of wealthy Americans. Once again, judgments were mixed. Twenty-three percent, for example, felt that the new rich had "more social conscience to do what's right" than earlier generations of wealthy people, 39 percent said that they had less, and 30 percent, about as much. About three in ten thought that the new rich contributed more to charity, 28 percent said that they contributed less, and 32 percent, about the same amounts.

A recent survey by Louis Harris and Associates reveals mixed assessments about a center of power and wealth, Wall Street. In the October 1997 poll, 80 percent thought that Wall Street, described as "the nation's largest banks, investment banks, stockbrokers and other financial institutions," benefited the country (27 percent a lot, 53 percent somewhat), and only 13 percent, that it harmed the country (10 percent somewhat, 3 percent a lot). Strong majorities of all educational, partisan, and racial groups agreed with this premise. Responding to a series of statements about Wall Street, 69 percent thought that Wall Street was absolutely essential because it provided the money business must have for investments, and 64 percent (in 1996) thought that most successful people there were highly intelligent. But note the ambivalence. At the same time, 56 percent stated that most people on Wall Street would be willing to break the law if they believed they could make a lot of money and get away with it, and 52 percent contended that Wall Street was dominated by greed and selfishness (table 2–8).

Given their own modest expectations, Americans think that people in many occupations are overpaid. An early survey suggests that this perception is deeply rooted. In a 1936 survey conducted for *Fortune* by Elmo Roper, respondents were asked, "Do you think that in general the officials of large corporations are paid too much or too little for the work they do?" Fifty-five percent said these individuals were paid too much, 17 percent volunteered that they were paid the right amount, and only 6 percent said that they were paid too little. The opinions of those categorized as "prosperous" were not dramatically different from those labeled as "poor." Fifty-one percent of the former and 57 percent of the latter said that officials of large corporations were paid too much.

Fifty-three years later, in 1989, Roper Starch Worldwide asked whether people in seventeen occupations were generally overpaid, underpaid, or paid about the right amount for what they do. Fifty-three percent of those surveyed said that presidents of major corporations were generally overpaid, 3 percent thought that they were underpaid, and 30 percent said that they were paid about the right amount. Thirty-eight percent said that U.S. senators and representatives were overpaid, 11 percent called them underpaid, and 39 percent thought that they were paid about the right amount.

In 1990, Roper asked about those particular occupations again, but the organization dropped most other occupations and added new ones, which the firm continues to inquire about today. Between 1989 and 1990, there was a twenty-two percentage point jump in the percentage of people who thought that CEOs were overpaid, with a twenty-seven point jump in those who thought that members of Congress were overpaid. The responses have not changed much since 1990.

In 1996, 90 percent felt that professional athletes were overpaid, 86 percent felt that way about celebrities and entertainers, 86 percent about lawyers, 79 percent about CEOs, and 68 percent about senators and congressmen. A strong majority, 57 percent, said that TV news anchors were overpaid, and 55 percent said that about investment bankers. Fifty-four percent saw senior-level managers in government as overpaid (table 2–9).

In the October 1997 Harris survey cited above, 51 percent thought that most successful people on Wall Street deserved to make the kind of money they earned, but 44 percent disagreed.

Our review of the small number of survey questions on CEO compensation turned up an especially striking finding. In September 1987, NBC News and the *Wall Street Journal* asked employed people about the income of the chief executive of their company. Only 28 percent contended that their CEO was paid too much; 12 percent, paid too little; and 44 percent, about the right amount. But 60 percent thought that executives of U.S. companies were paid too much, and 27 percent, about the right amount. Only 3 percent said that they were paid too little. A decade later, 29 percent in a May 1997 survey by Louis Harris and Associates said that the CEO of their company was paid too much; 10 percent, too little; and 47 percent, about the right amount. Seventy-five percent said top officers of large U.S. companies were paid too much (19 percent said that they were paid about the right amount, and just 3 percent, that they were paid too little.)

A September 1996 CBS News/*New York Times* survey of business executives found that a bare majority, 51 percent, felt that, in general, many chief executive officers were overcompensated. A third said that the compensation for most CEOs was appropriate.

The surveyors broke down the responses for executives of small, medium, and large companies. Fifty-two percent of those at small companies said that many CEOs were overcompensated (32 percent said that the compensation was appropriate), and 44 percent of those at medium-sized companies said that many were overcompensated (38 percent that the level was appropriate). Only a third of executives at large companies thought that many CEOs were overcompensated. Fifty-six percent of this group said that most CEOs received appropriate compensation.

To round out our survey of views about wealth, we looked at a discrete group of questions on wealthy political candidates whose personal fortunes were self-made or inherited. The public does not appear to resent either group. In several 1940 polls, people seemed unconcerned about Wendell Willkie's ties to a large electric utility company, although the questions do not make it clear whether respondents were reacting to his tie to a utility company or his earnings from it. Thirty years later, roughly six in ten disagreed that Nelson Rockefeller was too rich to be trusted. Perhaps surprisingly, in the intervening years we could find no questions about politicians' wealth or wealthy politicians. If pollsters' questions are a kind of rough gauge to issues on the minds of Americans, John F. Kennedy's Catholicism was a greater worry than was his wealth.

In a 1992 Gallup poll, people assessing Ross Perot stated that his opposition to the Persian Gulf War, his stand on abortion, and his inexperience in politics were more of a concern to them than his wealth. Sixty-six percent said his wealth would not influence their vote, 10 percent indicated that it would make them more likely to vote for him, and 22 percent, less likely. In a Harris poll, 58 percent rejected the argument that "it is wrong that Perot can spend $100 million or more to get himself elected;" just 39 percent agreed. In a bipartisan survey by the Tarrance

Group and Mellman Lazarus Lake, 60 percent thought that the description "too wealthy to understand my problems" did not accurately describe Ross Perot. Only 14 percent felt that this was a very good description. Throughout the 1992 presidential campaign, people told the pollsters that Perot's wealth would insulate him from the power of special interests.

Similar questions in 1996 about Perot and a few questions about Republican primary candidate Steve Forbes suggest that personal wealth is not a negative factor in politics. A comprehensive January 1997 *Washington Post* survey about campaign finance reform asked people what bothered them most about campaign financing. Of six reasons given, including things such as politicians who raise funds from outside their home states and politicians who raise funds from PACs, "wealthy candidates who use their own money to pay for their election campaigns" bothered people the least—only 22 percent expressed irritation about this. Roughly twice as many were bothered by the other two items mentioned here.

It is true that Americans *are* inclined to say that we have gone overboard in our attention to wealth and material comforts. Responding to a 1990 Gallup survey, 70 percent observed that too much emphasis and attention were centered on the rich and trying to become rich in America today. Only 6 percent said there was too little. But these responses seem almost perfunctory. In the 1995 Harwood Group survey for the Merck Family Foundation, 95 percent characterized most of their fellow Americans as materialistic, with a majority saying that most Americans were *very* materialistic. Those surveyed seemed particularly concerned about the materialism of today's young people.

In general, then, while many Americans are ambivalent about great wealth, few are hostile to it. This goes far to explain why disparities in wealth in this country have generated so little political heat.

TABLE 2–1
INCOME NEEDS FOR VARIOUS LIFESTYLES, SELECTED
YEARS, 1987–1996
(median in dollars)

Question: How much income per year do you think you
and your family. . . ?

	Need Just to Get By	Need to Live in Reasonable Comfort	Would Need to Fulfill All Your Dreams
1987	20,000	30,000	50,000
1989	20,000	30,000	75,000
1990	22,100	35,000	84,000
1991	25,100	35,100	83,800
1992	25,300	35,800	82,100
1993	23,700	35,500	100,300
1994	25,000	40,000	102,200
1995	25,500	41,000	102,000
1996[a]	30,000	40,000	90,000

NOTE: All responses are medians. These have not been adjusted
for inflation. The unadjusted numbers here show a 50 percent
increase from 1987–1996 in the "need just to get by" category, a
33 percent increase "to live in reasonable comfort," and an 80
percent increase "to fulfill all your dreams." The consumer
price index increased 38 percent from 1987 to 1996.
a. Sample is adults thirty years old and over.
SOURCE: Surveys by Roper Starch Worldwide (1987–1995) and
by the Roper Center for Public Opinion Research/University of
Connecticut for *Reader's Digest* (1996).

TABLE 2–2
Desirability and Likelihood of Becoming Rich, 1990, 1996, and 1997
(percent)

Question: All in all, if you had your choice, would you want to be rich, or not?

	Yes	No
May 1990	59	38
Sept. 1990	58	42
Apr. 1996	60	37
Men	65	32
Women	55	42
18–29 years	67	30
50+ years	46	50
<H.S. grad.	43	53
College grad.	70	27

Question: Looking ahead, how likely is it that you will ever be rich?

	Very Likely	Somewhat Likely	Not Very Likely	Not at All Likely
May 1990	9	23	32	35
Sept. 1990	9	19	27	45
Apr. 1996	10	24	37	27
Men	12	26	35	26
Women	9	22	39	28
18–29 years	18	46	30	6
50+ years	6	7	35	49
<H.S. grad.	5	13	39	38
College grad.	9	30	38	19
July 1997	11	25	28	33

SOURCE: Surveys by the Gallup Organization (May 1990; Apr. 1996); ABC News/*Washington Post* (Sept. 1990); Princeton Survey Research Associates (July 1997).

TABLE 2–3
COUNTRY BETTER OFF OR WORSE OFF
WITH NO RICH PEOPLE? 1942, 1979, AND 1992
(percent)

Question: Do you think the country would be better off or
worse off if we had no rich people? (*Fortune*)
Question: Everything considered, do you think society
would be better off or worse off if there were no millionaires? (RSW)

	Better Off	Worse Off	Don't Know
1942[a]	21	67	12
1979	24	51	25
1992	21	44	34

a. Sample is high school students.
SOURCE: Survey by Elmo Roper for *Fortune* (1942), and by
Roper Starch Worldwide (1979, 1992).

TABLE 2–4
CONCERN ABOUT THE NUMBER OF RICH PEOPLE, 1990
(percent)

Question: As far as you are concerned do we have too
many rich people in this country, too few, or about the
right amount?

Too many rich	21
Too few	15
About the right amount	55

SOURCE: Survey by the Gallup Organization, May 1990.

TABLE 2–5
IS GREAT WEALTH A BOON OR A CURSE FOR SOCIETY? 1990
(percent)

Question: Does America benefit from having a class of rich people or not?

Yes	62
No	32

NOTE: This question was asked of those people who did not consider themselves rich—1,249 of the 1,255 respondents.
SOURCE: Survey by the Gallup Organization, May 1990.

TABLE 2–6
DO THE WEALTHY HAVE TOO MUCH POWER AND INFLUENCE? 1979, 1982, AND 1992
(percent)

Question: Of course, the job of running the country is given to the President and Congress. However, there are those who say that other groups in our society also have power and influence over how our country is run. Would you call off the groups on that list that you feel have too much power and influence over our country's policies. . . the wealthy.

	Too Much Power/Influence	Rank
1979	58	2 of 23
1982	63	1 of 24
1992	45	1 of 26

NOTE: In 1979, the Arab oil nations ranked first as having too much power and influence over our country's policies. In 1989, large business corporations were ranked second, and, in 1992, the press was a close second to the wealthy.
SOURCE: Surveys by Roper Starch Worldwide, latest that of January 1992.

TABLE 2–7
PERCEPTIONS ABOUT MILLIONAIRES, 1992
(percent)

Question: Here is a list of things you may hear said about millionaires from time to time. Would you read down it and for each one tell me whether you think it is generally true or generally untrue of most millionaires?

	Generally True	Generally Untrue
Use their wealth mostly to protect their own positions in society	67	15
Don't pay their fair share of taxes	61	28
Investments create jobs and help provide prosperity	55	27
Favor the Republicans over the Democrats	55	14
Spending gives employment to a lot of people	54	29
Are politically conservative	53	24
Contribute generously to charitable causes	50	34
Worked hard to earn the wealth they have	46	37
Make illegal contributions to political campaigns	45	25
Got where they are by exploiting other people	38	35
Play too much and work too little	35	43
Really live no differently than most people, except they have more money	32	55
Keep the common man from having his proper share of the wealth	30	50
Feel a responsibility to society because of the wealth they have	29	47
Are responsible for many of society's ills	29	48

SOURCE: Survey by Roper Starch Worldwide, January 1992.

TABLE 2–8

PERCEPTIONS ABOUT WALL STREET, 1996 AND 1997

(percent)

Question: Please say if you tend to agree or disagree with the following statements about Wall Street?

	Agree	
	1996	1997
Wall Street is absolutely essential because it provides the money business must have for investments.	69	69
Most successful people on Wall Street are highly intelligent.	64	NA
Most people on Wall Street would be willing to break the law if they believed they could make a lot of money and get away with it.	64	56
Wall Street is dominated by greed and selfishness.	61	52
Wall Street only cares about making money and absolutely nothing else.	57	48
In general people on Wall Street are as honest and moral as other people.	43	51
Most successful people on Wall Street deserve to make the kind of money they earn.	40	51
We could close down Wall Street and most of the country would hardly notice.	21	NA

NOTE: In the 1996 survey, 70 percent thought Wall Street, described as "the nation's largest banks, investment banks, stockbrokers, and other financial institutions," benefited the country, and 22 percent thought it harmed the country. The percentages for the 1997 survey were 80–13.
SOURCE: Surveys by Louis Harris and Associates, latest that of October 1997.

TABLE 2–9
OCCUPATIONS: OVERPAID OR UNDERPAID? 1990 AND 1996
(percent)

Question: Now here is a list of people in different kinds of occupations. Would you go down that list and for each one tell me whether it is your impression that people in that occupation are generally overpaid, or underpaid, or paid about right for what they do?

	May 1990	May 1996		
	Overpaid	Overpaid	Underpaid	Paid about right
Professional athletes	82	90	1	8
Celebrities and entertainers	a	86	1	8
Lawyers	81	86	2	10
Presidents of major business corporations	75	79	1	15
U.S. senators and congressmen	65	68	3	23
Doctors	67	65	5	26
TV news anchor people	63	57	2	24
Investment bankers	a	55	2	24

Senior-level managers in the federal government	51	54	4	29
Middle-level managers in the federal government	39	42	7	35
Middle-level managers of major business corporations	a	26	11	49
Military officers	a	18	21	46
Nurses	7	6	56	33
Public school teachers	7	5	72	20
Policemen	4	5	62	27
Skilled factory workers	9	4	50	38
Secretaries	3	3	66	26
Restaurant workers	a	2	82	13

NOTE: In 1989, 53 percent said that the "presidents of major business corporations" were overpaid, 3 percent said underpaid, and 30 percent said that they were paid about the right amount. The figures for U.S. senators and representatives were 38 percent, 11 percent, and 39 percent, respectively.

a. Not asked.

SOURCE: Surveys by Roper Starch Worldwide, latest that of May 1996.

3

How Money Matters

In the United States, class divisions have been relatively weak. The historian Gordon Wood notes that, by the second decade of the nineteenth century, "Americans were already referring to themselves as a society dominated by the 'middling' sort."

"To be sure," he says,

> these terms were being used in England at the same time, but their significance in America was different. In England the term "middle class" had a more literal meaning than it did in America: it described a stratum of people who lay between the aristocracy and the working class. But in America, in the North at least, already it seemed as if the so-called middle class was all there was.[7]

A Middle-Class Country

In a 1940 survey for *Fortune*, Elmo Roper asked people, "What word would you use to name the class in America you belong to?" He identified 3 percent as upper class, 47 percent as middle class, and 15 percent as lower class. Six percent gave other answers, and 28 percent said that they did not know. In 1949, a National Opinion Research Center (NORC) survey found 2 percent describing themselves as lower class, 61 percent as working class, 32 percent middle class, and 3 percent upper class. The identical question was not asked again by NORC until 1972. In that year, the number considering themselves working class dropped, and the number considering themselves middle class rose. The numbers have been stable since then. In 1996, when NORC repeated the question, 6 percent called themselves lower class, 45 percent working class, 45 percent middle class, and 4 percent upper class (table 3–1).

Other survey organizations phrase the class question differently. CBS News in 1995 and the *Washington Post*, the Kaiser Family Foundation, and Harvard University in 1996 asked the identically worded question, "Do you consider yourself part of the middle class, or not?" Identical percentages of people (81 percent) answered they were.

A different perspective on class comes from a question ABC News and the *Washington Post* started to ask in 1981. It begins, "When asked, most people say that they belong to either the middle or the working class." On fourteen occasions, the surveyors have asked people what they would call themselves if they had to choose between the two. In each case, a majority has selected "working class," and roughly four in ten "middle class" (table 3–2).

A Gallup question that asked about people's financial class found most people (59 percent) describing themselves as middle income. Of 1,255 respondents in a 1990 survey, only 6 people (under 1 percent) identified themselves as rich. Seven percent described themselves as upper income. Twenty-three percent called themselves lower income, and 10 percent, poor. When Gallup repeated the question in April 1996, the responses were virtually identical. One percent described themselves as rich, 8 percent as upper income, 58 percent as middle income, 24 percent lower, and 9 percent poor. Majorities of Democrats (53 percent), Republicans (65 percent), and independents (57 percent) called themselves middle income, as did majorities of all ideological groups.

In the 1996 survey, a plurality (45 percent) of the income group below $15,000 called themselves lower income, 31 percent called themselves poor, and 23 percent of this group called themselves middle income. A plurality in the next income category ($15,000–19,999) said that they were lower income (45 percent), but more of this group called themselves middle income (37 percent) than poor (12 percent). Majorities of all groups above $20,000 described themselves as middle income. With the vast bulk of society describing itself as middle class, polarization is not pronounced.

Beginning in 1964, we have been able to locate four sets of questions that ask people about their family's class when they were young and then about their class today. The responses confirm the general middle-class orientation of the country. The questions also reveal intergenerational mobility. The response categories in these four sets of questions differ, but, in each case, the number considering themselves middle class when compared with their parents has risen (table 3–3).

A striking example of differences in attitudes in a more traditional hierarchical society with strong class divisions and our own with weaker class divisions comes from the responses in Britain and here to a question about whether people considered their society as divided into haves and have-nots. Every time the question has been asked in Britain, large majorities have said that their society was divided so. Equally large majorities in the United States responded that their society was not segmented this way (table 3–4). Hostility against wealth has little place to grow in a culture dominated by a vast middle class.

Satisfaction with Material Possessions

Surveys taken in 1989 and again in September 1996 by NBC News and the *Wall Street Journal* reveal another reason for a lack of resentment of wealth: most Americans feel that they have most of the things they need. In the 1996 survey, 38 percent responded that they and their families had "most of the material possessions" they needed (40 percent in 1989), and 41 percent said that they had "pretty much" of what they needed (37 percent in 1989). Seventeen percent in 1996 and 18 percent in 1989 answered that they had "only some" of the possessions they needed, and 4 and 5 percent, respectively, said that they had very little. In 1996, 67 percent of those in households with incomes of less than $20,000 said that they had most or almost everything they needed, as did 73 percent of households with annual incomes between $20,000 and $30,000.

In its 1996 survey for *Reader's Digest*, the Roper Center for Public Opinion Research asked, "In the past five years, was there ever anything that your family needed—not a luxury item, but a necessity—that you simply could not afford?" One-quarter of the sample (adults thirty years old and over) said yes, but three-quarters (74 percent) said no. When those who answered yes were asked what the family had needed but could not afford, 34 percent said a car, 12 percent health care or insurance, and 11 percent home repairs. Nothing else was volunteered by more than 10 percent. Those surveyed were then asked whether their families could not afford any necessity when they were growing up. Thirty percent said yes, but 68 percent said no. Those necessities that they could not afford were clothes (14 percent), food (14 percent), and a car (12 percent).

Needs and wants are different, as an August 1994 survey by Luntz Research Companies shows.

Thirty-five percent of respondents agreed that "I need more material things than my parents did at this time in their life" (64 percent disagreed). But 52 percent said that they *wanted* more than their parents did at this stage of their lives (47 percent did not).

Americans recognize improvements in their own and the nation's standard of living from their parents' time. Five times between 1989 to 1995, Cambridge Reports/Research International asked people to compare their standard of living with their parents'. The responses were stable. Each year, almost six in ten said that their standard of living was higher, while two in ten described it as lower. Roughly the same number described it as "about the same."

In the July 1996 survey for *Reader's Digest*, the Roper Center for Public Opinion Research asked adults thirty years old and over whether a family with a number of different possessions would be considered average in economic terms, slightly above average, or well above average. They then asked respondents how that family would have been seen "when you were a teenager." In each case, more people in their teen years than today believed that such a family was "well above average" (table 3–5).

In the same survey, people with children were asked if their children had more possessions than they had when they were young and whether the possessions were more costly, on average. Huge majorities, 85 and 93 percent, respectively, answered yes to both questions. Seventy-two percent said that their household goods—furniture, decorations, and gadgets— were worth more than those of their parents.

In this *Reader's Digest* survey, people were asked to think about their experiences in their teen years and compare them with their experiences today. Sixteen percent reported a vacation including an airplane trip in their teen years. Today, 51 percent had flown in an airplane while on vacation in the past three years. As teens, 7 percent had taken a vacation overseas. Today, three times as many (20 percent) say they have. A plurality (45 percent) reported that their family had one car when they were teens (32 percent said two); today a plurality (42 percent) say they have two, 14 percent say three, and 31 percent, one.

Nearly every survey we have been able to find shows that most Americans are generally satisfied with the material aspects of their lives and see improvements from the past.

The Importance of Wealth

A Roper Starch Worldwide question asked in 1975, 1985, and 1990 found that "being wealthy" ranked far down the list as a "personal idea of success," a finding echoed by many other surveys (table 3–6). In a survey in February 1995 by the Harwood Group for the Merck Family Foundation, substantial majorities identified responsibility (92 percent), family life (91 percent), friendship (85 percent), generosity (72 percent), and religious faith (66 percent) as important guiding principles in their lives. Far fewer, 37 percent, identified prosperity and wealth as such.

Gallup asked an extensive battery of questions in a 1990 survey about the advantages of wealth. The security wealth provided was its most attractive aspect; 81 percent said that not having to worry about affording unexpected expenses such as illnesses or emergencies was an important reason for wanting to be rich. The next group of responses dealt with actions such as being able to help one's children and being able to contribute to charity: 79 percent said being able to send children through college without financial strain was an important reason for wanting to be rich, 63 percent wanted to be able to contribute generously to charity, and 55 percent wanted to be able to pass money along to their children. Material goods ranked

far down the list as an advantage: only 8 percent
thought that owning expensive clothes was an important reason to want wealth; 10 percent said that owning an expensive car was, and 16 percent, a big house.

The 1995 Harwood Group survey found that
around one in five respondents saying that they would
be much more satisfied with their lives if they had a
nicer car (21 percent) or a bigger house or apartment
(19 percent). Far more expected greater satisfaction if
they could spend additional time with family (66 percent) and if they felt they were doing more to make a
difference in their communities (47 percent).

The old adage that money does not buy happiness
is supported by polling data. In both 1990 and 1996,
Gallup asked about the happiness of the rich: the
responses were virtually identical. Eleven percent in
both years supposed that rich people were happier
than the respondents were. Majorities, 50 and 52 percent, respectively, replied that both they and the rich
were equally happy. Slightly over a third in both years
(36 and 35 percent) said that the rich were less happy.
The 1990 Gallup survey on wealth also considered
what people would or would not willingly do to become
rich. Significant numbers said that they themselves
would be not very willing to work twelve–fourteen
hours every day of the year to become rich (47 percent), to work at a job they hated (72 percent), or to
spend little time with their family (80 percent).

The security that wealth can provide is undeni-
ably attractive. Yet again, given the general level of
contentment with material possessions and the place
of wealth in people's lives, enmity toward the wealthy
is unlikely. The July 1997 Princeton Survey Research
Associates/*Newsweek* poll about the new rich found
only 5 percent admitting that they resented most
wealthy people. Nineteen percent said that they
admired them, and 73 percent said that they did not
think much about them.

Reasons for Riches and Poverty

In 1986, James R. Kluegel, a sociologist at the University of Illinois, and Eliot R. Smith, a psychologist from Purdue University, published *Beliefs about Inequality: Americans' Views of What Is and What Ought to Be*.[8] They conducted a national survey (and a survey of Illinois residents) in which they investigated why Americans think some people are rich and why some are poor. The authors asked the national sample to rate the importance of a number of causes of wealth, including personal effort, ability or talent, political pull, inherited wealth, the unfairness of the economic system, dishonesty, and luck. Sixty-four percent selected "personal drive, willingness to take risks" and "money inherited from families" as "very important" reasons why "there are rich people in the United States." About as many, 60 percent, selected "hard work and initiative." Forty-seven percent chose "political influence or pull," and 46 percent, "great ability or talent." Significantly, only 29 percent selected as a very important reason that "the American economic system allows [the rich] to take unfair advantage of the poor," and 27 percent cited "dishonesty and willingness to take what they can get." Almost the same number (26 percent) mentioned good luck or being at the right place at the right time as very important. The individual and the structural reasons are not mutually exclusive, and many people selected both kinds of answers. But the average percentage for the explanations based on individual drive, ability, or pluck was higher than the average percentage for the explanations based on the structure of society.

The same pattern of giving great weight to individual achievement appeared in the data about why people are poor. The authors asked respondents to rate the importance of several individual causes for poverty (lack of thrift, lack of ability, lack of effort, attitudes that hold people back, and poor morals) and social ones (being taken advantage of by the rich, poor schools, low wages, and lack of jobs). Kluegel and Smith were able to compare their results with those from a 1969 survey. They concluded that people's view of what causes poverty has been remarkably stable over time. Once again, the average percentage selecting the individualistic reasons for poverty was higher (this time considerably higher) than the average percentage selecting the societal explanations.

In 1990, the National Opinion Research Center asked people to assess the importance of four reasons for the presence of poor people in this country. Two explanations related to the individual himself; two were structural. More people selected as very important the "lack of effort by the poor themselves" (45 percent) than selected any other reason. Only 8 percent indicated that this was not important as an explanation for poverty. Thirty-eight percent answered that loose morals and drunkenness were very important reasons; a quarter dissented. The results were similar for the structural response "failure of society to provide good schools for many Americans." This was cited as very important by 35 percent and not important by 24 percent. Thirty-five percent considered the failure of industry to provide enough jobs as very important, with 21 percent saying that this was not important.

In 1992, NORC asked a national sample about the importance of a long list of factors for "getting ahead in life." Ninety percent called "ambition" essential or very important, 88 percent felt that way about hard work, 87 percent about having a good education, and 52 percent about natural ability. Fewer selected "knowing the right people" (43 percent) and "having well-educated parents" (41 percent). Much smaller percentages mentioned "coming from a wealthy family" or "having political connections" (18 percent), "being born a man or a woman" (17 percent), a person's race or religion (15 percent), or a person's political beliefs (11 percent).

Other survey explorations of the reasons for wealth and poverty are less subtle than Kluegel and Smith's and NORC's, but they reinforce Americans' emphasis on individual responsibility for circumstances. In 1972, for example, the University of Michigan's National Election Study asked people to agree or disagree with this statement: the poor are poor because the American way of life does not give all people an equal chance. Thirty-eight percent agreed, but 59 percent disagreed. In its 1990 survey on wealth, Gallup asked people which of two things was "more often the cause if a person is rich—strong effort to succeed on his or her part, or luck or circumstances" beyond the individual's control? Fifty percent responded that it was strong effort, and a third, luck or circumstances.

Since 1964, Gallup has occasionally asked which is more often to blame if a person is poor: lack of effort by the individual or circumstances beyond his control. In nearly every survey, a significant number of people have volunteered the response "both," suggesting that they feel uncomfortable with the stark choice being presented in the question (table 3–7). The identical question has been asked in Britain since 1971. In the last four iterations (1986, 1989, 1992, and 1994) fewer than two in ten in Britain have selected the response "lack of effort." In Britain, where class boundaries are still strong, more people than in the United States choose the response of circumstances beyond one's control. In the last four queries, majorities have given this response.

A battery of questions asked by NORC sheds more light on public views about social differences in the United States. In 1984 and again in 1990, NORC asked respondents to agree or disagree with this statement: "Only if differences in income and social standing are large enough is there an incentive for individual effort." In 1984, 56 percent agreed; 38 percent disagreed. In 1990, those figures were 52 and 37 percent. In 1984, a robust 72 percent agreed that differences in social standing between people are acceptable because they basically reflect what people have made out of their opportunities. Twenty-five percent disagreed. Seventy percent in 1992 agreed that no one would study for years to become a lawyer or doctor unless they expected to earn much more than ordinary workers; 20 percent disagreed.

More people disagreed than agreed in 1987, 1992, and 1996 that large differences in income are necessary for America's prosperity. In response to another question, 52 percent stated that, all in all, social differences in the country are justified

Unsurprisingly, given the emphasis that people place on individual effort and talent as sources of achievement, admiration for those who become rich by working hard is widespread. In four surveys conducted by the Pew Research Center in the 1990s, nearly nine in ten said they agreed with the statement "I admire people who get rich by working hard." In each survey, majorities or near majorities *completely* agreed with the statement (table 3–8).

Beliefs about Opportunity

Historian Oscar Handlin has described the core of the American experiment:

> Opportunity is the one prize a free society has to offer. It assures individuals the scope within which to make the most of their abilities, and it permits the community to profit from the appropriate use of talent where it is most advantageous. In that sense opportunity endows a society with justice. Everyone gains

when the race for position goes to the swiftest, the winner from having ambition fulfilled, everyone else from having services performed by the best qualified.[9]

The American idea of equality—one that distinguishes it to this day from other nations—is rooted in the notion of equality of *opportunity*. The equality of opportunity quickly provided by the new nation meant that people would move up and down the economic ladder and that class and other distinctions would not harden over time. The idea appears indelibly stamped on American minds, as shown by the results of a 1993 NORC question, "Some people think America should promote equal opportunity for all, that is, allowing everyone to compete for jobs and wealth on a fair and even basis. Other people think that America should promote equal outcomes, that is, ensuring that everyone has a decent standard of living and that there are only small differences in wealth and income between the top and bottom in society." A robust 84 percent favored the standard of equal opportunity, while only 12 percent favored equal outcomes. Perhaps because the ideal has been taken for granted, pollsters—until recently—rarely bothered to inquire about it.

In 1939 survey work for *Fortune*, in a rare early question about opportunity, Elmo Roper asked his national sample whether their opportunities to succeed were better or worse than their parents' opportunities. He also asked whether their sons' opportunities to succeed would be better or worse than their own. Strong majorities were optimistic about their own and their sons' opportunities. In 1946, Gallup asked fathers and mothers about their sons' and daughters' opportunities to succeed. Fathers' and mothers' responses were similar. Sixty-four percent of fathers expected their sons to have better opportunities; only 13 percent, not as good ones. Sixty-one percent of mothers anticipated better opportunities for their daughters; 20 percent, worse.

For the next forty years, no survey organization paid much attention to our beliefs about opportunity. This attitude began to change in the early 1980s, and today pollsters often ask about it. One explanation for the new interest is the extraordinary growth spurt in the polling business in the 1970s. This development contributed to an increase in the number of polls conducted and the kinds of topics explored. Another possible explanation for this new attention to beliefs about opportunity is that the mirror that pollsters hold to society reflects anxiety about opportunity— something that pollsters would naturally want to explore. Given the centrality of the concept of equal opportunity to how we define ourselves, any perceived erosion of that idea would be serious.

In addition to concerns about opportunity, there are worries about the American dream. A common refrain in much political and journalistic commentary today is that the American dream is in danger, that its demise is imminent. Supposedly, at some earlier time, the idea of the American dream was robust.

But that case cannot be made with public opinion polls. The first reference to the "American dream" in the Roper Center historical archive of polls does not appear until 1983, and it is not even explicitly in the question. ABC News and the *Washington Post* asked: "All of us want certain things out of life. When you think about what really matters in your own life, what are your wishes and hopes for the future? In other words, if you imagine your future in the best possible light, what would your life look like then if you are to be happy. . . ?" Slightly over one-third mentioned something about financial security, 32 percent mentioned good health, and 21 percent pointed out concerns about their happiness or their children's happiness. The interviewers cobbled together a hodge-podge of responses about happy marriage, home ownership, and children into a category they coded as the American dream, mentioned by 15 percent of those surveyed. We simply do not know how people would have answered questions about the dream in the past because they were not asked. Drawing sweeping conclusions from data that extend back barely more than a decade is unwarranted. We return to a discussion of data about the American dream on page 39.

Throughout the history of polling, survey researchers have asked questions about whether people expected to be better or worse off in the next year or in the next few years. These questions were essentially referendums on current economic performance, and the answers were positive or negative depending on current conditions. In the spring and summer of 1997, the answers to these questions were more positive than they had been in years. In December 1997, the Conference Board reported the highest level of consumer confidence in twenty-eight years. In July 1997, the University of Michigan's Index of Consumer Sentiment reached 107, its highest level since the mid-1960s. Had we written this monograph in early 1994, 1995, or 1996, we would have painted a more negative picture of people's views of their economic well-being.

Questions about current economic conditions and expectations for the next year or two may be important, but they do not speak to the underlying values that we are trying to understand here. Thus, we have not included these kinds of questions in this monograph.

What do available data tell us about the health of the core idea of opportunity? We begin with an examination of a series of questions about hard work and opportunity.

1. Whenever a question presents opportunity in the context of hard work, large majorities say that opportunity is present for those who are willing to work hard. The questions in table 3–9 are roughly comparable, and, although they are few in number, they have the advantage of having been asked over a period of forty-five years. The results show no significant diminution in the belief that opportunity is present for those willing to work hard. Majorities disagree with the view that hard work offers little guarantee of success (table 3–10). Cross-national surveys show just how unique the United States is on this point. In the 1990–1993 World Values Survey, 59 percent in the United States placed themselves at points 1–3 on the ten-point scale, where point 1 represented the belief "in the long run, hard work usually brings a better life," and point 10 represented "hard work doesn't generally bring success; it's more a matter of luck and connections." By contrast, only 38 percent in hierarchical Britain and 33 percent in tradition-bound Japan took this view (see appendix). Few in the United States (9 percent) could be found at points 8–10, supporting the belief that "hard work doesn't usually bring success; it is more a matter of luck and connections."

2. Solid majorities surveyed over fifteen years contended that it was still possible to start out poor, work hard, and become rich. In 1990, a majority maintained that a person had a very good or good chance of becoming rich through hard work, although 46 percent said that there was some or little chance. Only 2 percent thought that there was no chance of this occurring (table 3–11).

3. When people are asked to compare themselves to their parents, virtually every question we have been able to locate finds that majorities, usually strong ones, say that they are better off today—better off in terms of opportunity, preparation for adulthood,

standard of living, quality of life, finances, income, homes, and lifestyle and material possessions—no matter how the question is asked (tables 3–12 — 3–18).

4. The picture is less clear when people are asked to compare their lives with what they think their children's lives will be like. When people are asked about their own children, they are usually more optimistic than pessimistic. They are also generally more positive about their own children than about the next generation as a whole (tables 3–12 and 3–15 — 3–25). When the Roper Center for Public Opinion Research asked a long series of questions in 1996 about opportunity, standard of living, and finances, people were consistently positive about their own lives compared with their parents'. They were also optimistic about their own children. When asked about the next generation, however, they were more pessimistic than optimistic (table 3–18).

Reconciling some findings is hard. Consider the questions about standard of living. A Cambridge Reports/Research International question asked between 1989 and 1995 found 43–52 percent saying that *their* children's standard of living would be higher than their own and only about two in ten saying that it would be lower. Around three in ten said that it would be the same (table 3–15). The 1996 findings of the Roper Center for Public Opinion Research were similar: 53 percent expected *their own* children to have a higher financial standard of living than they had, 12 percent a lower one, and 29 percent about the same (table 3–18). The *Los Angeles Times*, in a question asked since 1991, consistently finds significant numbers expecting the *next* generation to have a worse standard of living than now. Between 13 and 24 percent have expected it to be better, and around a third said that it would be about the same (table 3–21). These responses support the supposition offered above: people are more positive about their own offspring than they are about the next generation as a whole.

But NBC News and the *Wall Street Journal* also ask people about *their own* children. Unlike the other questions discussed in this paragraph, this query does not offer a middle category. The yes and no response categories, no doubt, affect responses. On each of the four occasions in 1996 when the question was asked, responses were more negative than positive. In April and June 1997, however, bare majorities expected their children's standard of living to be higher than their own (table 3–20), suggesting that the answers to this question, perhaps more than some of the others we display, are a proxy for people's view of current economic conditions and not a statement of their views about their children's long-term prospects.

Two questions about opportunity asked over a long time span produce different impressions. Both asked people about their children. A Roper Starch Worldwide question on view in table 3–12 shows a decline from 1939 to 1993 in optimism about "your [son's/children's] opportunities," though the responses are still more positive than negative (49 to 32 percent in the latest available question from 1993). A Gallup question, asked in 1946 and 1997, finds no change in fathers' positive views about their sons' opportunities but a sizable increase in mothers' optimism about their daughters' opportunities. Eighty-five percent of mothers in 1997, compared with 61 percent in 1946, felt that their daughters' opportunities would be better than theirs (table 3–12).

A question posed by Roper Starch Worldwide does not use the "better/worse" formulation but asks instead how confident people are that life for their children will be better than it has been for them. In 1973, 26 percent were very confident that their children's lives would be better than their lives. By 1995, that figure had slipped to 17 percent. In 1973, 30 percent were not at all confident that their children's lives would be better than theirs; in 1995, that figure was 34 percent. Opinion had risen unevenly in the middle category, "only fairly confident," from 36 to 44 percent (table 3–25).

5. In his *Political Dictionary,* William Safire writes that the term *American dream* "defies description as much as it invites discussion."[10] Both observations are borne out by the polls. In 1992, Wirthlin Worldwide asked a question about the meaning of the American dream to which people could give any response they wanted. Nine percent, the highest response given, mentioned freedom. That year Wirthlin and Roper Starch Worldwide each asked about the idea's personal meaning. Wirthlin asked respondents to place, on a scale of 1 to 10, attributes representing their sense of the American dream. Good health and financial security in retirement were above 9; true love, rewards for hard work, and a family placed above 8. College graduation and car ownership followed, at 7.9, and marriage and community service, at 7.6. A high-paying job was at 7.5 on the dream scale; winning the lottery, at 4.8. The Roper Starch Worldwide question found that a happy relationship was a "very important element" in the American dream for 90 percent of respondents, a family was for 84 percent, friends who respect you mattered to 83 percent, and being one of the best in your job was crucial to 80 percent. The next category cited as a very important element was making or doing something useful for society. In a 1994 survey, Luntz Research Companies asked whether believing in God was part of the American dream. Eighty-four percent said that it was. It is probably not advisable to place too much weight on individual questions about it. The findings that we discuss next underscore this point.

Surveys about the American dream—and they are few in number and generally quite recent—show that reports of its death have been exaggerated (table 3–26). Of course, people's answers about whether it is still possible to attain the American dream differ depending on the wording of questions. Table 3–27 shows that, in response to a 1996 ABC News survey, 71 percent thought that most people could still achieve the American dream. But a Yankelovich Partners series (also displayed in the table) finds majorities in three recent askings saying that the dream has become impossible for most people to achieve. An Opinion Dynamics survey for Fox News in February 1997 asked about the dream in the context of hard work: "Do you think that if an individual works hard, they can still achieve the American Dream of making a decent living, owning a home, and sending their children to college?" Seventy-two percent said yes, 24 percent no. Another survey conducted in February 1997, this one by Peter Hart and Robert Teeter for the Council for Excellence in Government, found 30 percent responding that, in today's society, the American dream was achievable for all Americans willing to work for it; 29 percent felt that it was achievable for most; 24 percent said it was achievable only for some; and 16 percent, for very few Americans, even if they were willing to work for it. These results were similar to those obtained when pollsters asked the same question in 1995. In the next question in the 1997 survey, however, 65 percent said that they were already living the American dream, but 28 percent said they had not been able to do so (table 3–27).

In a November 1996 survey by Luntz Research Companies, 20 percent responded that they had already achieved the American dream, 46 percent that they were close, 21 percent very far away, and 9 percent said that they never expected to experience it. In a 1995 bipartisan survey by the Tarrance Group and Mellman Lake Lazarus, 14 percent described themselves as very close to achieving their version of the American dream, 41 percent said that they were close, 18 percent somewhat far, and 12 percent very far. In this survey, 8 percent volunteered that they had already achieved it, and 2 percent stated that they did not have a personal version of the American dream. A Wirthlin Worldwide question asked in 1992 and 1995 found majorities in both years reporting that their parents had achieved the dream. Larger majorities expected that their children, or the next generation, would. Fewer than two in ten said that they themselves would not achieve the dream, and a substantial number in both years said that they had already achieved it (table 3–27). The general picture from such questions shows more optimism than pessimism about personal prospects for the dream, though people say that the dream is harder to attain than in the past and that it will be harder to attain in the future (table 3–28).

Which of the many different questions asked about opportunity or the American dream should we trust? Are the questions that remind people of their own experience compared with the past, let's say, their parents' generation, more valid than those that ask about expectations for the amorphous next generation? Should we rely more on questions about things people know best—themselves and their own families—or do we get a clearer assessment of the state of the nation when people are asked about all Americans or the next generation? Similar issues come up over and over again in survey research. Which should we trust more—people's views about their own congressman (generally positive) or Congress as a whole (more negative), their views about their own doctor (highly positive) or their views about the medical profession (generally more negative)? Should we place more weight on people's views of the present than on their musings about the future? Are the negative responses about the prospects for the next generation an echo from adversarial and negative media, or is something deeper occurring? If people are becoming more pessimistic about the country, we might expect to see the evidence in responses about their children's prospects: here the data are murky.

People are generally good judges of their own situation, and thus we put more weight on how they describe their own lives than how they describe the well-being of their fellow Americans. Even taking into account normal parental anxiety about one's own offspring, most people are probably better judges of their own children's prospects than of the prospects of most children. Many polls these days pick up a negativity or "pop" cynicism about society as a whole that is pervasive. In a kind of vicious circle, the ubiquitous polls regurgitate the cynicism common in the culture.

A polling exercise illustrates the point. In 1945, the word *lie* was used for the first time in a survey question. From the early 1970s through President Nixon's resignation in 1974, it was used four times. During the Iran-contra investigation in 1986–1987, *lie* was used in survey questions eighty-eight times. The pejorative *politics as usual* was used three times in the 1940s, not again until the 1970s, and several dozen times in 1997 to describe Democratic and Republican fund-raising practices. We can find no references to a politician "hiding something" before 1988.[11] Most observers of our politics would probably agree that politics is cleaner than twenty, thirty, or fifty years ago and that the propensity of politicians to lie is unlikely to have changed much over time. Yet the impression gleaned from the poll-infused media is a much more negative one than we would have experienced years ago. What Americans say about most politicians or most Americans is likely to be informed and colored by a media culture that accentuates the negative. Thus, we are skeptical of questions that are not anchored in actual experience.

In the November 1996 round-table discussion at AEI, Stanley Greenberg and Guy Molyneux cautioned that there is a reason to pay close attention to per-ceived views of most Americans as well as personal attitudes. Molyneux argued that people want to feel good about their own situation, particularly male respondents who often see themselves as breadwin-ners. He argued that it was hard for them "to tell an interviewer that they are doing a lousy job providing for their families." He concluded that people do not tell pollsters that their own wages and salaries are too low when questions are phrased that way. Greenberg argued "most people think they are—often by heroic efforts—doing a good job supporting their families." But, he added, they think that "living standards for average Americans are stagnant." In their personal optimism, he found "a critique of what is happening to average Americans," a critique that contains the seeds of a politics that may make concerns about inequality resonate more strongly.

Being middle class, Greenberg argued, "repre-sents at one level a view of household income, but it also represents the idea of people who are working hard, taking personal responsibility, living by the rules, and trying to support their families." These peo-ple, he stated, "feel that they are not honored today and that they are playing by a harder set of rules than others in society." The issue is not, he continued,

> CEOs making more money, it is CEOs making more money while downsizing and layoffs are occurring. It is not about having wealth, it is about having wealth at the expense of people who are working hard and trying to do better

for their families. It is not about punitive taxation or redistribution; it is about achieving a society consistent with the norms of working class Americans. What is happening to average Americans, he says, violates the norm of fairness and leads people to be more sensitive to inequality issues such as the power and tax burdens of various groups.

Is Greenberg onto something? This question occupies us in the next chapter.

TABLE 3–1
HOW WE CLASSIFY OURSELVES,
SELECTED YEARS, 1949–1996
(percent)

Question: If you were asked to use one of these four names for your social class, which would you say you belong to— the lower class, working class, middle class, or upper class?

	Lower	Working	Middle	Upper
1949	2	61	32	3
1972	6	47	44	2
1973	4	48	46	3
1974	4	47	46	3
1975	5	48	44	3
1976	4	46	48	2
1977	4	49	43	4
1978	5	47	45	2
1980	5	46	45	3
1982	5	48	44	3
1983	6	47	44	4
1984	5	46	46	3
1985	4	45	47	4
1986	6	43	44	3
1987	5	43	47	4
1988	5	45	47	2
1989	5	43	48	4
1990	4	46	47	3
1991	5	43	49	2
1993	7	45	45	3
1994	5	45	46	3
1994[a]	4	31	59	4
1996	6	45	45	4

a. In a 1994 survey for *Reader's Digest*, the Roper Center inadvertently changed the order in which the classes were given. It began the question with "the middle class" and followed it with lower class, working class, and upper class. The order in which the categories were read may explain the differences in the responses. SOURCE: Surveys by the National Opinion Research Center (1949–1996) and the Roper Center for Public Opinion Research/University of Connecticut for *Reader's Digest* (1994).

TABLE 3–2
MIDDLE CLASS OR WORKING CLASS?
SELECTED YEARS, 1981–1996
(percent)

Question: When asked, most people say that they belong
to either the middle class or the working class. If you
had to make a choice, would you call yourself middle
class or working class?

	Middle Class	Working Class
July 1981	42	55
May 1982	37	59
Sept. 1982	44	53
July 1983	43	53
June 1985	43	55
July 1986	38	57
Mar. 1992	46	52
July 1992	45	55
Oct. 1994	47	52
Mar. 1995	41	58
July 1995	45	54
Oct. 1995	43	55
Mar. 1996	43	56
Aug. 1996	45	53

SOURCE: Surveys by ABC News/*Washington Post*, latest that of
August 1996.

LADD AND BOWMAN ◆ 47

TABLE 3–3
INTERGENERATIONAL MOBILITY,
SELECTED YEARS, 1964–1996
(percent)

Question: Thinking back to the time you were growing up, would you say that your family was of the upper class, upper middle class, middle class, working class, or lower class?

	Lower	Working	Middle	Upper Middle	Upper
Oct. 1964	5	45	38	9	3

Question: By and large, do you think of yourself as being of the upper class, upper middle class, middle class, working class, or lower class?

	Lower	Working	Middle	Upper Middle	Upper
Oct. 1964	3	37	45	11	2

Question: How would you describe your family when you were growing up: lower class, working class, middle class, or upper class?

	Lower	Working	Middle	Upper
Apr. 1978	18	46	31	3

Question: Well, if you were asked to use one of four names for your social class, which would you say you were in: the lower class, the working class, the middle class, or the upper class?

	Lower	Working	Middle	Upper
Apr. 1978	8	44	43	2

(Table continues)

TABLE 3–3 (continued)

Question: We hear a lot about different classes in this country—the middle class, for example. All things considered, in which of these classes would you place your parents—the lower class, the lower middle class, the middle class, the upper middle class, or the upper class?

	Lower	Lower Middle	Middle	Upper Middle	Upper
June 1984	6	19	51	19	2

Question: All things considered, in which of these classes would you place yourself—the lower class, the lower middle class, the middle class, the upper middle class, or the upper class?

June 1984	4	20	57	16	2

Question: How about your family back when you were a teenager, in what class would you place your family back then?

	Lower	Lower Middle	Middle	Upper Middle	Upper
July 1996[a]	18	26	40	13	2

Question: In what economic class would you place yourself—lower class, lower middle class, middle class, upper middle class, or upper class?

July 1996[a]	6	23	48	19	2

a. Sample is adults thirty years old and over.
SOURCE: Surveys by the National Opinion Research Center (1964), CBS News/*New York Times* (1978), Roper Starch Worldwide (1984), and the Roper Center for Public Opinion Research/University of Connecticut for *Reader's Digest* (1996).

TABLE 3–4

AMERICAN-BRITISH COMPARISON: HAVES AND HAVE-NOTS,
SELECTED YEARS, 1984–1994

(percent)

Question: Do you think of [America/Britain] as divided
into haves and have-nots, or don't you think of
[America/Britain] that way?

Year	Country	Yes	No
1984	U.S. response	31	61
1984	British response	63	33
1986	British response	67	27
1988	British response	73	23
1988	U.S. response	26	71
1990	British response	72	23
1992	British response	70	21
1994	British response	75	20

SOURCE: Surveys by the British Gallup Organization, except for
the 1984 U.S. response, which was a survey by CBS News/*New
York Times,* and the 1988 U.S. response, which was a survey by
the Gallup Organization.

TABLE 3–5
WEALTH TODAY COMPARED WITH TEEN YEARS, 1996
(percent)

Question: In terms of wealth, would a family today with . . .
be considered average, slightly above average, or well above
average? How about back when you were a teenager?

	Average	Slightly above Average	Well above Average
Two relatively new cars			
Today	47	38	14
When you were a teenager	15	18	65
A home and a vacation cottage			
Today	13	41	45
When you were a teenager	8	15	75
That goes on an overseas vacation every summer			
Today	7	19	74
When you were a teenager	4	9	85
Owns a 20-ft. sailboat			
Today	11	35	52
When you were a teenager	6	16	76
Owns a swimming pool			
Today	43	42	13
When you were a teenager	12	28	58

NOTE: Sample is adults thirty years old and over.
SOURCE: Survey by the Roper Center for Public Opinion
Research/University of Connecticut for *Reader's Digest*, 1996.

TABLE 3–6
PERSONAL IDEAS OF SUCCESS, 1975, 1985, AND 1990
(percent)

Question: Which comes closest to expressing your personal idea of success?

	1975	1985	1990
Being a good wife and mother or husband and father	43	37	42
Being true to yourself	38	39	36
Being true to God	35	32	32
Having friends that respect you	23	21	21
Making/doing things that are useful to society	17	20	15
Being knowledgeable and well informed	16	18	14
Being wealthy	**6**	**12**	**13**
Having power and influence	5	9	8
Being prominent or famous	3	3	5

SOURCE: Surveys by Roper Starch Worldwide, latest that of July 1990.

TABLE 3–7

THE CAUSE OF POVERTY, SELECTED YEARS, 1964–1997
(percent)

Question: In your opinion, which is more often to blame
if a person is poor—lack of effort on his own part, or circumstances beyond his control?

	Lack of Effort	Circumstances	Both[a]
Mar. 1964	34	29	32
Sept. 1964	34	25	38
Nov. 1964	31	31	34
Oct. 1965	40	27	27
Dec. 1965	40	29	28
May 1967	42	19	36
Apr. 1968	41	28	29
Mar. 1982	37	39	17
Dec. 1984	33	34	31
July 1988	40	37	17
Aug. 1989	38	42	17
May 1990	35	45	17
Dec. 1990	30	48	20
Feb. 1992	27	52	18
Dec. 1994	44	34	18
Dec. 1995	35	42	18
Nov. 1997	39	44	14

a. Volunteered response. Question wording varies slightly
(1990–1994).
SOURCE: Surveys by the Gallup Organization (Mar. 1964–May
1967; Dec. 1984–May 1990); National Opinion Research Center
(Apr. 1968); CBS News/*New York Times* (Mar. 1982; Dec.
1994–Dec. 1995); *New York Times* (Dec. 1990); the *Los Angeles
Times* (Feb. 1992); and Princeton Survey Research Associates
for the Pew Research Center for the People & the Press (Nov.
1997).

TABLE 3–8
ADMIRATION FOR PEOPLE WHO GET RICH
BY WORKING HARD, SELECTED YEARS, 1992–1997
(percent)

Question: I am going to read you a series of statements about a number of different things. For each, please tell me whether you completely agree with it, mostly agree with it, mostly disagree with it, or completely disagree with it . . . I admire people who get rich by working hard.

	Completely Agree	Mostly Agree	Mostly Disagree	Completely Disagree
1991	57	35	5	2
1992	47	42	7	3
1994	51	37	8	3
1997	52	37	7	3

NOTE: Question wording varies slightly.
SOURCE: Surveys by Princeton Survey Research Associates for the Times Mirror Center for the People & the Press (1991–1994) and for the Pew Research Center for the People & the Press (1997).

TABLE 3–9
HARD WORK AND OPPORTUNITY,
SELECTED YEARS, 1952–1997
(percent)

Question: Some people say there's not much opportunity in America today—that the average man doesn't have much chance to really get ahead. Others say there's plenty of opportunity, and anyone who works hard can go as far as he wants. How do you feel about this?

	Yes, There's Opportunity	*No, There's Little Opportunity*
1952	87	8

Question: How good a chance do you think a person has to get ahead today, if the person works hard?

	Very Good / Good Chance	*Some / Little Chance*	*No Chance at All*
1980	63	35	2

Question: (Agree/disagree) America is the land of opportunity where everyone who works hard can get ahead?

	Strongly Agree / Agree	*Disagree / Strongly Disagree*
1980	70	31

Question: A basic American belief has been that if you work hard you can get ahead—reach the goals you set and more. Does that still hold true?

	Yes, Still True	*Not True*
1994	74	24

TABLE 3–9 (continued)

Question: Please tell me whether you strongly agree, somewhat agree, somewhat disagree, or strongly disagree with the following statement: In America, if you work hard, you can be anything you want to be.

	Strongly / Somewhat Agree	Somewhat / Strongly Disagree
1994	74	25

Question: "In America, if you work hard, you can be anything you want to be," do you strongly agree, somewhat agree, somewhat disagree, or strongly disagree?

	Strongly / Somewhat Agree	Somewhat / Strongly Disagree
1996	80	20

Question: People who work hard in this nation are likely to succeed?

	True	False
1997	79	18

SOURCE: Surveys by the University of Michigan National Election Survey (1952), Kluegel and Smith, *Beliefs about Inequality: Americans' Views of What Is and What Ought to Be* (1980 survey for 1986 book), the Roper Center for Public Opinion Research/University of Connecticut for *Reader's Digest* (1994), Luntz Research Companies (1994, 1996), and Opinion Research Corporation for *USA Weekend* (1997).

TABLE 3–10
HARD WORK AND SUCCESS, SELECTED YEARS, 1987–1997
(percent)

Question: Now I am going to read to you a series of statements that will help us understand how you feel about a number of things. For each statement, please tell me if you completely agree with it, mostly agree with it, mostly disagree with it or completely disagree with it . . . Hard work offers little guarantee of success.

	Completely / Mostly Agree	Mostly / Completely Disagree
May 1987	29	68
May 1988	32	66
Feb. 1989	41	57
May 1990	36	63
Nov. 1991	44	54
Jan. 1992	41	56
Feb. 1992	42	56
Mar. 1992	45	52
May 1992	42	57
June 1992	32	66
Sept. 1992	45	52
July 1994	39	60
Nov. 1997	33	66

SOURCE: Surveys by the Gallup Organization for Times Mirror Center for the People & the Press (1987–1989) and by Princeton Survey Research Associates for Times Mirror/Pew Research Center for the People & the Press (1990–1997).

TABLE 3–11
POSSIBILITIES OF STARTING OUT POOR, BECOMING RICH,
SELECTED YEARS, 1981–1996
(percent)

Question: Do you think it's possible to start out poor in this country, work hard, and become rich?

	Yes, It's Possible	No, It's Not Possible
Apr. 1981	67	28
Jan. 1983	57	38
Feb. 1996	70	27
Mar. 1996[a]	78	18

Question: How good a chance do you think a person has to become rich today, if the person is willing to work hard?

	May 1990
Very good/good chance	51
Some/little chance	46
No chance at all	2

NOTE: Question wording in 1981 varied slightly. The results included the voluntary response "possible through other means" (2 percent).
a. CBS News only.
SOURCE: For top panel, surveys by CBS News/*New York Times*, latest that of March 1996. For bottom panel, survey by the Gallup Organization, May 1990.

TABLE 3–12
OPPORTUNITIES TO SUCCEED, SELECTED YEARS, 1939–1997
(percent)

Question: Do you think your opportunities to succeed are better than, or not as good as, those your parents had? Question: Do you think your [son's/children's] opportunities to succeed will be better than, or not as good as, those you have? (If no children:) Assume that you *did* have children. (RSW)

	Better	Not as Good	Same [a]
Your opportunity to succeed compared with your parents			
Dec. 1939[b]	61	20	12
Feb. 1940[b]	59	22	13
Jan. 1947[b]	70	13	13
Dec. 1990	70	15	12
Aug. 1993	63	22	11
Your [son's/children's] opportunity to succeed compared with yours			
Dec. 1939[b]	61	15	10
Feb. 1940[b]	60	15	10
Jan. 1947[b]	62	13	12
Dec. 1990	61	21	12
Aug. 1993	49	32	10

TABLE 3–12 (continued)

Question: (Asked of mothers) Will your daughter's opportunities to succeed be better than or not as good as those you've had?
Question: (Asked of fathers) Will your son's opportunities to succeed be better than or not as good as those you've had? (Gallup)

	Better	Not as Good	Same
Mother's opinions of daughter's opportunities to succeed			
1946	61	20	12
1997	85	7	6
Father's opinions of son's opportunities to succeed			
1946	64	13	13
1997	62	21	11

a. Volunteered response.
b. Question asked only about father's/son's opportunities to succeed. In this question asked of married people without sons, people were asked to assume they had a son. Single women were not asked this question.
SOURCE: For first two panels, surveys by Roper Starch Worldwide, latest that of August 1993. For second two panels, surveys by the Gallup Organization, latest that of February 1997.

TABLE 3–13
BETTER PREPARED TO GET AHEAD THAN PARENTS,
1939 AND 1990
(percent)

Question: Do you think you are better or less prepared to get ahead than your parents were?

	Better	Less	Same [a]
1939	72	9	13
1990	76	10	10

a. Volunteered response.
SOURCE: Surveys by Roper Starch Worldwide, latest that of December 1990.

TABLE 3–14
OPPORTUNITIES FOR AMERICANS COMPARED WITH THE PAST,
SELECTED YEARS, 1983–1996
(percent)

Question: Since the time this country was settled, the United States has been called the land of opportunity. Do you think there are more opportunities for Americans today than in the past, or less opportunities today, or about the same today as in the past?

	More	Fewer	About the Same
Jan. 1983	40	34	25
Jan. 1985	52	20	25
June 1986	54	21	22
Oct. 1986	49	24	26
Jan. 1990	47	20	28
Mar. 1996[a]	41	27	30

a. Question wording varied slightly. It asked if there were fewer opportunities today.
SOURCE: Surveys by Roper Starch Worldwide (Jan. 1983–Jan. 1990) and CBS News (Mar. 1996).

TABLE 3–15
COMPARING GENERATIONS ON STANDARD OF LIVING,
1989 AND 1992–1995
(percent)

Question: Do you think your standard of living is higher, lower, or about the same as your parent's standard of living? Now, looking into the future, do you think your children's standard of living will be higher, lower, or about the same as your standard of living?

	Higher	*Lower*	*About the Same*
Your standard of living is . . .			
1989	59	19	20
1992	59	19	21
1993	57	18	23
1994	55	20	24
1995	58	20	21
Your children's standard of living will be . . .			
1989	52	12	19
1992	47	15	28
1993	49	17	27
1994	43	22	28
1995	46	17	29

NOTE: Category "don't have children" not shown above.
SOURCE: Surveys by Cambridge Reports/Research International, latest that of January 1995.

TABLE 3–16
COMPARING GENERATIONS' QUALITY OF LIFE,
1994 AND 1996
(percent)

Question: How does your generation's quality of life compare with your [parent's generation/children's genera-
tion]? Is it much better, somewhat better, somewhat
worse, much worse or about the same?
Question: How does your generation's standard of living
compare with your [parent's generation/children's gener-
ation]? Is it much better, somewhat better, somewhat
worse, much worse or about the same?

	Better	Worse	Same
Your generation's . . . compared with your parents' generation			
1994			
Quality of life	64	22	13
Standard of living	68	19	13
1996[a]			
Quality of life	74	21	3
Standard of living	74	22	3
Your generation's . . . compared with your children's generation			
1994			
Quality of life	44	16	31
Standard of living	49	20	26
1996[a,b]			
Quality of life	48	44	4
Standard of living	48	45	4

NOTE: Categories combined.
a. Question wording does not include the "about the same"
option.
b. Compares *next generation's* quality of life/standard of living
to your own rather than *your children's* quality of life/standard
of living.
SOURCE: Surveys by Luntz Research Companies, latest that of
November 1996.

TABLE 3–17
COMPARING GENERATIONS' FINANCIAL SITUATION,
SELECTED YEARS, 1980–1996
(percent)

Question: Think of your parents when they were your age. Would you say you are better off financially than they were or not?

Question: And what about your children? Do you think they will be better off than you are financially when they reach your age, or not? (For people who say they have no children, ask: "Suppose you did have children, do you think those children would be better off financially or not when they reach your age?")

	Are Better Off than Parents at Your Age	Not Better Off than Parents at Your Age
Apr. 1980	88	10
Mar. 1981	64	35
Dec. 1981	69	28
Mar. 1982	69	30
Jan. 1983	70	29
Nov. 1983	77	21
Dec. 1983	73	25
Jan. 1985	74	23
Mar. 1985	75	23
Mar. 1986	81	18
Apr. 1986	78	21
May 1986	82	17
May 1991	70	26
Jan. 1995	67	31
Jan. 1996	67	30
Mar. 1996	70	29
May 1996	69	29

(Table continues)

TABLE 3–17 (continued)

	Children Will Be Better Off at Your Age	Children Will Not Be Better Off at Your Age
Mar. 1981	47	43
Mar. 1982	43	41
Jan. 1983	44	45
Nov. 1983	62	27
Dec. 1983	65	29
Jan. 1985	62	29
Mar. 1986	74	19
Apr. 1986	69	26
May 1986	71	23
May 1991	66	25
Jan. 1995	54	39
Jan. 1996	52	39
Mar. 1996	52	42
May 1996	60	33

SOURCE: Surveys by ABC News/*Washington Post*, latest that of May 1996.

TABLE 3–18
EXPECTATIONS AND ACCOMPLISHMENTS, 1996
(percent)

Question: Do you agree or disagree with the following: in America today, people like me (and my family/spouse) have a good chance of improving our standard of living?

Agree	Disagree
70	27

Question: Considering your entire adult life, do you think you've gotten ahead financially, fallen behind financially, or stayed about the same?

Gotten Ahead	Fallen Behind	Stayed Same
54	18	29

Question: Is your financial standard of living—which includes your houses and lifestyles as well as your income—higher than your parents achieved during their peak financial years, lower, or about the same?

Higher	Lower	About the Same
56	22	21

Question: Considering income, as well as homes and lifestyles, do you think that your generation is enjoying a higher economic standard of living than your parents' generation, a lower economic standard of living, or about the same as your parents' generation?

Higher	Lower	About the Same
64	16	19

(Table continues)

TABLE 3–18 (continued)

Question: All in all, are you (and your spouse) better off financially than your parents were when they were your age, about the same, or worse off financially than your parents were when they were your age?

Better	Worse	About the Same
59	17	21

Question: Some people say although there are many economic hardships faced by every generation in America, eventually most will do better financially than their parents. Thinking about your own generation, do you think it is true that eventually most people in your generation will do better financially than their parents or not?

Will Do Better	No, Most Will Not Do Better
70	23

Question: Do you feel that you, personally, will eventually do better financially than your parents, or not?

Yes	No
70	19

Question: Do you think that by the time they are your age, your children will have a higher financial standard of living than you have now, a lower one, or about the same?

Higher	Lower	About the Same
53	12	29

Question: Do you think the average American family is better off now economically than the average American family forty years ago, meaning the 1950s, or not?

Better Off Now	Better Off in the 1950s
59	31

TABLE 3–18 (continued)

Question: How about compared to twenty years ago, meaning the 1970s?

Better Off Now	Better Off in the 1970s
46	38

Question: Do you think the next generation will be better off financially or worse off financially than the current generation?

Better	Worse Off	About the Same [a]
29	52	8

NOTE: Sample is adults thirty years and over.
a. Volunteered response.
SOURCE: Survey by the Roper Center for Public Opinion Research/University of Connecticut for *Reader's Digest*, 1996.

TABLE 3–19
LIKELIHOOD FOR TODAY'S YOUTH OF BETTER
LIFE THAN PARENTS, SELECTED YEARS, 1983–1996
(percent)

Question: In America, each generation has tried to have a better life than their parents, with a better living standard, better homes, a better education, etc. How likely do you think it is that today's youth will have a better life than their parents—very likely, somewhat likely, somewhat unlikely, or very unlikely?

	Very Likely	Somewhat Likely	Somewhat Unlikely	Very Unlikely
Jan. 1983	19	35	27	17
Jan. 1985	28	40	19	10
Jan. 1990	21	41	20	13
Oct. 1992	28	46	13	4
Dec. 1995	11	38	32	17
July 1996	16	42	27	13
Sept. 1996	16	42	27	13
Oct. 1996	11	40	32	14
Nov. 1996	15	41	27	15
Dec. 1996	14	37	30	17

Question: Do you expect that your children will have a better life than you have had, a worse life, or a life about as good as yours?

	Better	Worse	About as Good
1989	59	10	25
1992	31	28	37
1996	50	16	26

SOURCE: For top panel, surveys by Roper Starch Worldwide (1983–1992); *New York Times* (Dec. 1995; Dec. 1996); and CBS News/*New York Times* (Sept. 1996–Nov. 1996). For bottom panel, surveys by Louis Harris and Associates, latest that of February 1996.

TABLE 3–20
YOUR CHILDREN'S GENERATION'S STANDARD OF LIVING,
SELECTED YEARS, 1990–1997
(percent)

Question: Do you expect your children's generation to enjoy a higher standard of living than your generation?

	Yes	No
May 1990[a]	60	37
July 1994	45	50
Sept. 1994	49	45
Dec. 1994	48	46
Mar. 1995[b]	49	45
Jan. 1996	41	52
Mar. 1996	41	51
June 1996[a]	43	47
Sept. 1996[a]	43	47
Apr. 1997	52	44
June 1997	53	42

a. Registered voters.
b. Council for Excellence in Government.
SOURCE: Surveys by NBC News/*Wall Street Journal* and Hart/Teeter Research for the Council for Excellence in Government.

TABLE 3–21
STANDARD OF LIVING FOR NEXT GENERATION,
1991–1996
(percent)

Question: Do you expect the next generation of Americans will have a better standard of living than the one we have now, a worse standard of living than now or about the same standard of living as we have now?

	Better	Worse	Same
Nov. 1991	20	51	23
Oct. 1992	24	36	36
Jan. 1993	23	38	35
June 1993	14	51	32
Dec. 1993	15	47	35
Oct. 1995	13	51	33
Aug. 1996	18	46	33

SOURCE: Surveys by *Los Angeles Times*, latest that of August 1996.

TABLE 3–22

EXPECTATIONS FOR FUTURE GENERATIONS, 1989–1997
(percent)

Question: Do you think the future generation of Americans will be better off, worse off, or about the same as people today?

	Better	Worse	Same
June 1989	25	52	18
June 1990	28	36	31
Mar. 1991	36	26	35
Oct. 1991	20	52	25
Nov. 1991	26	43	28
Sept. 1992	22	46	21
Oct. 1992	26	44	20
Nov. 1992[a]	30	35	30
Dec. 1992	25	40	31
Feb. 1993	22	49	22
Aug. 1994	32	46	18
Nov. 1994	18	57	21
Dec. 1994	21	47	30
Mar. 1995	16	58	20
Aug. 1996	16	48	31
Sept. 1996	24	38	32
Oct. 1996	31	34	33
Nov. 1996[a]	30	34	36
Feb. 1997	14	51	31

NOTE: Question wording varies slightly.
a. Sample is national adult voters leaving the polls.
SOURCE: Surveys by CBS News/*New York Times* (June 1989–Oct. 1992; Dec. 1992–Feb. 1993; Nov. 1994–Sept. 1996), Voter Research and Surveys (a consortium of ABC News, CBS News, NBC News, Cable News Network) (Nov. 1992), Luntz Research Companies (Aug. 1994), ABC News (Oct. 1996), Voter News Service (a consortium of ABC News, CBS News, Cable News Network, Fox News, NBC News, Associated Press) (Nov. 1996), and CBS News (Feb. 1997).

TABLE 3–23
CHILDREN'S FUTURE ECONOMIC SITUATION, 1986 AND 1997
(percent)

Question: In the future, what do you think the economic situation will be for your children or other people's children? Do you think they will be better off than you and your generation or worse off?

	Better Off	Worse Off
1986	48	39
1997	27	67

SOURCE: Surveys by Yankelovich Partners, latest that of February 1997.

TABLE 3–24
FUTURE FOR YOUR CHILDREN, MOST CHILDREN, 1994 AND 1996
(percent)

Question: Looking to the future, when your children grow up do you think they will be better off or worse off than you are now? Looking to the future, do you think MOST children in this country will grow up to be better off or worse off than their parents?

	Better	Worse	Same [a]
Your children[b]			
1994	47	39	5
1996	51	41	4
Most children			
1994[c]	33	50	6
1996	38	55	3

a. Volunteered response.
b. Based on sample of parents with children under 18.
c. Based on sample of nonparents only.
SOURCE: Surveys by Princeton Survey Research Associates for *Newsweek* (1994) and the Pew Research Center for the People & the Press (1996).

TABLE 3–25
CONFIDENCE ABOUT LIFE FOR YOUR CHILDREN,
SELECTED YEARS, 1973–1995
(percent)

Question: Now, taking some specific aspects of our life, we'd like to know how confident you feel about them. First, do you feel very confident, only fairly confident, or not at all confident that life for your children will be better than it has been for us?

	Very Confident	Only Fairly Confident	Not at All Confident
1973	26	36	30
1974	25	41	28
1975	23	39	32
1976	31	39	25
1979	25	41	29
1982	20	44	32
1983	24	38	33
1988	20	45	28
1992	17	46	31
1995	17	44	34

SOURCE: Surveys by Roper Starch Worldwide, latest that of September 1995.

TABLE 3–26
THE AMERICAN DREAM, ALIVE OR DEAD,
SELECTED YEARS, 1986–1996
(percent)

Question: I'd like to talk with you now about a term with which you are probably familiar—the American Dream. Do you personally feel that the American Dream is very much alive today, somewhat alive, or not really alive?

	Very Much Alive	Somewhat Alive	Not Really Alive
1986	32	55	11
1990	23	50	20
1992	16	52	26
1993	20	50	22
1995	22	52	21

Question: Do you think that the American Dream is very much alive today, somewhat alive today, or is it dead?

	Very Much Alive	Somewhat Alive	Dead
1994	23	64	12
1996	20	66	11

SOURCE: For top panel, surveys by Roper Starch Worldwide, latest that of December 1995. For bottom panel, surveys by Luntz Research Companies, latest that of November 1996.

TABLE 3–27
IS THE AMERICAN DREAM STILL POSSIBLE? 1992–1997
(percent)

Question: Do you think it's still possible for most people in this country to achieve the American Dream, or do you think that's not possible anymore? (ABC News)

	Still Possible	Not Possible
1996	71	26

Question: Do you think that if an individual works hard, they can still achieve the American Dream of making a decent living, owning a home, and sending their children to college? (OD/FN)

	Yes	No
1997	72	24

Question: Do you agree or disagree . . . The American Dream has become impossible for most people to achieve? (Yank.)

	Agree	Disagree
1995	57	40
1996	63	34
1997	55	41

(Table continues)

TABLE 3–27 (continued)

Question: In today's society, do you think the American Dream is achievable for all Americans who are willing to work for it; for most Americans, but not all; only for some Americans; or for very few Americans, even if they are willing to work for it? (H/T)

	All	*Most*	*Only Some*	*Very Few*
1995	33	29	22	15
1997	30	29	24	16

Question: Do you think you will reach, as you define it, "the American Dream" in your lifetime, or have you already reached it? Did your parents reach "the American Dream?" Your children, or the next generation, do you feel they will reach "the American Dream?" (WW)

	Aug. 1992	*Dec. 1995*
Have already reached the American Dream	37	45
Will reach it in my lifetime	43	35
Will not reach it in my lifetime	17	16
Parents reached the American Dream	54	55
Did not	43	39
Your children, the next generation, will reach	62	59
Will not	29	26

TABLE 3–27 (continued)

Question: And how close are you to achieving your own version of the American Dream? Have you achieved it already, are you close to achieving it, are you very far away, or do you never expect to achieve your version of the American Dream? (Luntz)

	Achieved It	Close	Very Far Away	Never Expect
1994	22	49	19	6
1996	20	46	21	9

Question: Do you feel that you have lived the American Dream or have been unable to live the American Dream? (H/T)

	Have	Have Not
1997	65	28

SOURCE: For top panel, survey by ABC News, May 1996. For second panel, survey by Opinion Dynamics/Fox News, February 1997. For third panel, surveys by Yankelovich Partners, latest that of January 1997. For fourth panel, surveys by Hart/Teeter Research for the Council for Excellence in Government, latest that of February 1997. For fifth panel, surveys by Wirthlin Worldwide, latest that of December 1995. For sixth panel, surveys by Luntz Research Companies, latest that of November 1996. For seventh panel, survey by Hart/Teeter Research for the Council for Excellence in Government, February 1997.

TABLE 3–28
THE AMERICAN DREAM COMPARED WITH THE PAST,
LOOKING TO THE FUTURE, SELECTED YEARS, 1986–1996
(percent)

Question: Compared with the past—say a generation
ago—do you feel the American Dream is easier to attain
today, harder to attain, or is it about the same?
Question: Looking to the future—say a generation from
now—do you feel the American Dream will be easier to attain
than today, harder to attain, or will it be about the same?

	Easier to Attain	*Harder to Attain*	*About the Same*
Compared with past			
Oct. 1986[a]	23	45	32
Dec. 1990	17	61	18
May 1992	8	72	18
Dec. 1993	13	64	19
Dec. 1995	12	63	22
Looking to future			
Oct. 1986[a]	10	55	33
Dec. 1990	13	62	19
July 1993	6	67	24
Dec. 1993	8	64	21
Aug. 1994[b]	14	78	4
Dec. 1995	8	66	20
Aug. 1996[c]	4	68	24
Nov. 1996[b]	16	77	4

a. In 1986, questions were asked of the 87 percent of respondents who believed the American Dream still had meaning. A
special analysis found that the difference in the bases had a neg-
ligible impact on the results, which are now based on the total.
b. Question wording varied and did not include the option of
"about the same." Four percent volunteered it none the less.
c. Question wording varied slightly.
SOURCE: For first group, surveys by Roper Starch Worldwide.
For second group, surveys by Roper Starch Worldwide (Oct.
1986; Dec. 1990; Dec. 1993; Dec. 1995), Princeton Survey
Research Associates for *Family Circle* (July 1993), Luntz
Research Companies (Aug. 1994; Nov. 1996), and CBS
News/*New York Times* (Aug. 1996).

4

Is the Ground Shifting?

The concerns that Greenberg and Molyneux raised about fairness are important. Equality of opportunity *is* a demanding standard. People must believe that our system is generally fair for it to remain vital. If this belief no longer exists—either because of changes in people's thinking about the economy and their place in it or because of changes in perceptions of the behavior of corporate America or the wealthy—the political repercussions could be significant.

We begin with a look at underlying perceptions about the economy. Are they changing in such a way as to make fairness issues more salient? If people are especially anxious economically, they may be more sensitive to disparities in wealth. Greenberg noted that people tell the pollsters that they are doing fairly well by their own families. Many survey questions support this view. Roper Starch Worldwide has asked people since 1974 how they are getting along and finds that roughly two-thirds say that they are getting along all right or fairly well (table 4–1). Replies to Gallup, NORC, and ABC News/*Washington Post* questions since 1974 show scant concern about the likelihood of losing a job in the next year (table 4–2). In December 1995 and again in December 1996, the *New York Times* asked a specific question about job layoffs. The interviewers said that they did not mean "temporary or seasonal lay-offs." The interviewers wanted information about "people losing their jobs due to employer downsizing, reductions-in-force, corporate restructuring, permanent plant closings, jobs moving overseas, or jobs just permanently disappearing." Twenty percent in 1995 and 25 percent in 1996 said they had experienced that kind of layoff "in the past 15 years." Of those who had this kind of experience, 50 percent reported that they had been laid off from one job, around 25 percent from two jobs, and slightly under 10 percent from three.

A battery of questions asked nine times between January 1996 and December 1997 by NBC News and the *Wall Street Journal* showed large majorities (61 percent in January 1996, 78 percent in December 1997) very or somewhat satisfied with their job security. Between March 1996 and December 1997, 60 percent or more were very or somewhat satisfied with their opportunities for career advancement.

Gallup surveys for *Inc.* magazine in November 1995 and January 1997 found high employee satisfaction with their place of employment. Over 80 percent in both years felt that their supervisor cared for them as a person and that percent said their own opinions seemed to count. Eighty percent in 1995 considered their company family-friendly (this question was not asked in 1997). When asked in 1995 and 1997, "From your most objective viewpoint, have you been compensated fairly this past year?" nearly seven in ten said that they had been. When the *New York Times* asked in 1995 and again in 1996 about personal finances in the past couple of years, about two in ten reported that they had been getting ahead financially, and slightly more than a quarter in both polls said that they had been falling behind. A majority said that they were staying even. In the 1996 survey, 48 percent reported being "at least as well off financially today" as they expected to be at that point in their lives, while 49 percent said that they were not. Those results resemble the ones obtained by the survey firm Research & Forecasts in an identical question asked in July 1984: 50 percent said that they were at least as well off, and 48 percent said that they were not.

Other polls reveal anxiety. Greenberg noted that the question asked by Roper Starch Worldwide in table 2–1 shows a 50 percent increase in a seven-year time frame in the amount of money people think it takes "just to get by." Large majorities in most polls know someone who has been laid off or has been a victim of downsizing. The most recent iteration of the Roper Starch Worldwide question, cited in table 4–1, finds a quarter saying that they "feel quite pinched" and 6 percent that they are "just not able to make ends meet" (table 4–1). Responding to a question asked since 1992 by several different survey organizations, four in ten Americans say they now earn enough money to lead the kind of life they want, but majorities do not. When those not earning enough to lead the kind of life that they want are asked a follow-up question about whether they will be able earn enough to lead such a life, however, more say that they will than not (table 4–3).

The widespread belief that two earners are needed today to make ends meet may be contributing to anxiety about the economy, though the wording of a question can produce different impressions in this area. In the 1996 survey by the Roper Center for Public Opinion Research of adults thirty years old and older, two-thirds of households with two or more people working full- or part-time said that more than one person had to work "to maintain the standard of living [they] desire[d]." A smaller, but still significant, 44 percent in the poll said that more than one person needed to work to *cover the family's basic necessities* (52 percent disagreed). Replying to a question asked by Chilton Research for the Kaiser Family Foundation, the Harvard University Survey Project, and the *Washington Post* in 1996, 87 percent believed that "in order to make a comfortable living," the average family must have two full-time wage earners.

In the November 1996 AEI session, Guy Molyneux argued that most people will tell a pollster that they are not in danger of losing their job any time soon. What has changed, he contended, is "their sense of the consequences of losing their job." They have very little confidence, he stressed, "that they could go out and find a comparably good job." Molyneux maintained that people are resigned to the belief that their wages will not increase much and, for that reason, the possibility of loss of or cutbacks in health care or retirement benefits becomes a greater concern. Even though people will say that their standard of living is as good as or better than their parents, he continued, they "don't feel they have the same kind of job security their parents had."

In the Kaiser/Harvard/*Washington Post* survey, 81 percent called themselves middle class. Of this group, about four in ten said that they had felt in danger of falling out of the middle class. In December 1995 and again in December 1996, the *New York Times* asked people about their social class. In December 1996, 3 percent called themselves upper class, 40 percent middle class, 47 percent working class, and 8 percent lower class. Of those who called themselves middle class, about one-third said that they had felt at risk of falling out of the middle class, but two-thirds had not. About one-third of those who called themselves working class said that they had felt in danger of falling out of the working class.

NBC News and the *Wall Street Journal* asked respondents nine times between January 1996 and December 1997 about their level of satisfaction with their retirement security. The number saying they were satisfied hovered around 50 percent; dissatisfaction was in the mid-40s. From January 1996 through December 1997, about four in ten were satisfied with the money that they were saving; majorities were dissatisfied.

In our discussion of opportunity and the American dream, we noted the disjunction between people's responses about themselves and their responses about most people, with the former being generally positive and the latter negative. The same pattern appears when people are asked how they are doing and when they are asked about how the middle-class or average Americans are faring. A majority in a survey done by Yankelovich Partners in 1994 described things as worse for the middle class these days; only 8 percent said that they are better (table 4–4).

Surveyed in late July–early August 1996 by Chilton Research for the Kaiser Family Foundation, the Harvard University Survey Project, and the *Washington Post*, a large majority (70 percent) believed that, "during the past 20 years," family incomes for average Americans had been falling behind the cost of living, while 19 percent said that they were staying even, and 11 percent that they were going up. Seventy-one percent replied that the wages of average Americans during the past twenty years had been falling behind the cost of living; 21 percent, that they had been staying even; and only 7 percent, that they had been going up. A 1996 survey conducted by Princeton Survey Research Associates for Knight Ridder newspapers found that only 12 percent felt "middle-class families" were better off than ten years ago (49 percent said they were worse off, and 39 percent about the same). When asked about "people like you," 24 percent said that they were better off, 27 percent worse off, and 47 percent about the same.

Scholars who have examined the data described

in this section draw different conclusions from them. University of Virginia sociologist James Davison Hunter designed a large-scale survey in 1996 (the fieldwork was done by Gallup) for the university's postmodernism project. In discussing the results in the *Public Perspective*, Hunter argued that the middle classes on the whole are not especially worried about the national economy, the local economy, about their jobs or their personal finances. Rather what they fear and what upsets them is the sense that everything they have lived for—their Judeo-Christian God, their family life, their moral commitments, their work ethic, and the public school system that would pass their beliefs on to their children—is in decline and possibly disappearing. It is not a "fear of falling" [out of the middle class] that haunts the middle classes, but a fear of the curtain falling upon their way of life.[12]

Greenberg went further, arguing that many people in the middle class today believe that they are playing by a harder set of rules than others in the society. In the past, he said, these people felt that they were being taken advantage of by those underneath them who were making gains at their expense. Today, they feel that they are being taken advantage of or squeezed by those above them. Greenberg contended that there is growing awareness of corporate excess today, making it possible that the public could become more sensitive to widening inequality.

We noted at the beginning of this section that the political fallout could be significant if people's perceptions about their place in the economy were changing negatively. Social unrest and demands for protectionism and for tax policies designed to soak the rich could follow from a deeply dissatisfied public. But the data that we have reviewed are not clearly negative or positive.

We also suggested the possibility of political repercussions if people's perceptions of the behavior of the rich or corporate America were becoming more negative. To reiterate what Greenberg said, the issue is not CEOs making more money. The issue is CEOs making more money while they are downsizing or laying off people. The issue is not having money, but using the power that comes with money to minimize tax burdens while people in the middle class who are working hard and playing by the rules get no such breaks.

Public attitudes in this area are hard to evaluate for a number of reasons. First, because few questions that might reveal new sensitivities about the wealthy or about corporate America are asked and few have trends, knowing whether anything is changing is difficult. We noted earlier the widespread belief that people in many occupations are overpaid, a conviction that has risen for CEOs and congressmen in the single trend question available. We also noted the ambivalence about wealth generally, an ambivalence that dampens the political intensity of concerns that people are overpaid.

The data about the fairness of our system are hard to evaluate for other reasons. Some questions that have been asked for a long time and that bear on economic inequality have become clichés, and it is unclear what political force they have. The belief, for example, that the rich do not pay their fair share of taxes is strong and steady. We do not think that we have ever seen a survey in which people say that the wealthy pay too much or even the right amount in taxes. Seventy-five percent in 1977 and 72 percent in 1992, in response to Roper Starch Worldwide questions, said that high-income families pay too little in taxes (table 4–5). An ABC News survey from 1987 that examined complaints about the tax system found overwhelming agreement (74 percent) with the statement that many rich people pay hardly any taxes at all.[13]

In a March 1995 survey conducted by Yankelovich Partners for *Time* and CNN, roughly three-quarters answered that the present tax system benefited the rich and was unfair to ordinary working men and women. The answers were similar to those given twenty years ago in response to a Harris question (table 4–6). About three-quarters in a Gallup poll for *Newsweek* in 1993 stated that wealthy Americans found loopholes to avoid paying their fair share of taxes. Only about two in ten said that the wealthy paid their fair share. Almost the same number gave that response in a 1987 *Washington Post* poll. Once again, however, it is hard to know whether people are more sensitive about these issues than in the past.

Another example of this generalized suspicion of the rich can be seen in questions about budget agreements. Since the 1980s, at least, people have told the pollsters that the rich, not themselves, will benefit from budget agreements. It does not seem to matter what the contents of an agreement are or whether they are negotiated by Republican or Democratic administrations; the response seems to be automatic. Absent intense media attention that might occur during a debate about a major restructuring of the tax system or an election campaign, however, it is not clear that people think much about how much the rich or poor pay in taxes or who will come out on top in a budget deal.

Other kinds of questions about the rich and the poor show little change over time. In 1984 and again in 1990, the Gallup Organization asked a national sample whether the percentage of Americans who were rich was increasing or decreasing from year to year. In both years, people said that their numbers were increasing. Since 1972, Louis Harris and Associates has been asking people whether they feel that "the rich get richer and the poor get poorer." Two-thirds or more have consistently agreed (table 4–7). In

1937 and twice in the 1960s, Gallup asked people whether poverty would ever be done away with in this country. Each time, roughly nine in ten answered that poverty would always be with us. In 1984, Harris asked a variant of the question; 85 percent stated that the country would not see an end to poverty. In 1989, replying to a Gallup question, 92 percent said that poverty would always be a major problem for society (table 4–8).

Individual topics in public opinion cannot be evaluated in isolation, and this is another reason why attitudes about fairness are hard to evaluate. Even if there is a new skepticism about corporate America or the wealthy, it is not clear that this trumps other contemporary attitudes, such as broad criticism of the performance of the federal government, that may be more politically consequential.

A survey by pollster Ethel Klein for the Preamble Center for Public Policy—an organization that describes its purpose as "to fight the neo-liberal economic policy consensus that has come to dominate the national political debate, and to develop and promote ideas for restricting the overwhelming power that corporations wield over virtually every aspect of American life"—included provocative questions that seemingly confirm a new skepticism about business.[14] The ideologically driven survey began in a straightforward way by asking people to grade corporations on actions such as paying good wages (36 percent gave corporations an A or B; 36 percent, a C; and 19 percent, a D or F), making quality products (53 percent, A or B; 31, C; 12, D or F), being loyal to employees (26, 28, 42), making profits (78, 9, 5), and keeping jobs in America (28, 31, 20).

The poll then inquired whether a series of corporate practices were serious problems and whether government should be doing something about them.

Fifty-eight percent found that corporations not providing health care and pensions to employees was a
serious problem that government should take action
about; 24 percent said that this was a serious problem
but government should not take action; and 18 percent, that it was not a serious problem. The responses
for "corporations laying off large numbers of workers
even when they are profitable" were 54, 27, and 19
percent, respectively. Responding to "corporations not
paying employees enough so that they and their families can keep up with the cost of living," 52 percent
called for government action; 24 percent, no action;
and 24 percent saw no serious problem. A final area of
inquiry, "corporations paying CEOs two hundred
times what their employees make," produced these
percentages: 48, 31, and 21. In each of these areas,
majorities or near majorities stated that the problems
were serious and that government ought to take
action, but majorities or near majorities replied either
that the problems were serious but government
should not be involved or that the problems were not
serious.

Responding to a December 1995 *New York Times*
poll—which became part of a series of articles about
economic anxiety—47 percent thought that government should step in and do something about layoffs
and the loss of jobs (46 percent, no). When the paper
repeated the question in December 1996, a slightly
larger number, 51 percent, said that government
should do something (39 percent, no).

Many survey questions show that people are far
more concerned today about problems associated with
big government than they used to be and also that
they are generally more skeptical of big government
than of big business. On twenty-two occasions since
1959, pollsters have asked which posed the biggest
threat to the country in the future: big business, big

labor, or big government. In 1959, 14 percent fingered big government; 41 percent, big labor; and 15 percent, big business. A decade later, in 1968, the numbers were 46 percent for big government as the biggest threat, 26 percent for big labor, and 12 percent for big business. In 1995, the percentage selecting big business had doubled (to 24 percent), and the percentage choosing big labor had sharply declined (to 9 percent). But the biggest threat by far in the public mind was big government, cited by 64 percent. Although big business is not blameless in the public's eyes, big government seems to be a more consequential villain. Suffice it to say that there is much criticism to go around, but criticism of government today, and particularly the federal government, is especially potent.

In the November 1996 discussion at AEI, Greenberg argued that, at different times, the middle class has worried about being squeezed by those underneath them and by those at the top making gains at their expense. According to the pollster, middle-class people today feel that they are being squeezed by those at the top. The poll data in the public domain do not provide clear evidence either way. Four times since 1992, *Los Angeles Times* pollsters have asked which is the bigger current problem for the country: people on welfare getting benefits that they do not deserve or the rich not paying their fair share of taxes. The public clearly does not like being forced to make a choice. Each time, roughly a third have named both as the problem. But, of the rest, more have said that those on welfare—and not the rich— are the problem. Replies to another question, framed differently, suggest that the middle class is being squeezed more by tax breaks for big business than by welfare programs (table 4–9).

Recent questions show awareness of an income gap, but scant trend data are available. In several

Roper Starch Worldwide surveys in the 1970s and two in the 1980s, slightly more than 35 percent said that the differences between the haves and the have-nots would increase. Around 15 percent in a separate question said that this posed a serious threat to our society and our way of life (table 4–10). A more recent question, posed in terms of the American dream, found 38 percent of those surveyed agreeing that differences between the haves and have-nots posed a serious threat to our society and way of life.

In 1994, 64 percent in a Yankelovich Partners poll for *Time* and CNN said that the income gap between the rich and poor in this country was widening. About twenty-five percent thought that it was not changing much, and only 6 percent said that it was shrinking. In late November and early December 1995, Princeton Survey Research interviewers (in a survey for the Kaiser Family Foundation, the Harvard University Survey Project, and the *Washington Post*) asked, "Compared with 20 years ago, do you think the difference in income between wealthy and middle-class Americans today is wider, not as wide or about the same?"

Sixty-five percent said that it was wider; 11 percent, not as wide; and 22 percent, about the same. A January 1997 Opinion Research Corporation/Gannett News Service survey was less straightforward. In response to the question, 36 percent said that we would always have rich and poor and that the gap between the two has not changed. A majority, 53 percent, replied that the gap between the rich and poor was increasing and creating more problems, and 8 percent, that the gap was narrowing and making things better.

Taken together, these data do not provide clear evidence that people's perceptions about their place in the economy or about the rich and corporate America are becoming sharply negative. Beyond this, the survey data are not adequate to tell us whether people think that society is less fair than it was ten, twenty, or thirty years ago.

TABLE 4–1
How Families Are Making Out, Selected Years,
1974–1995
(percent)

Question: Considering your income and what you have to
live on and the cost of living, how would you say your
family is making out today—all things considered would
you say you are getting along all right, or getting along
only fairly well, or feeling quite pinched, or just not able
to make ends meet?

	All Right	Fairly Well	Quite Pinched	Not Making Ends Meet
Nov. 1974	25	41	28	6
Feb. 1975	24	40	27	9
Apr. 1975	32	39	22	7
May 1975	27	38	25	9
June 1975	28	41	25	6
Nov. 1975	27	39	26	7
Jan. 1976	27	42	24	6
June 1976	28	41	23	6
Jan. 1977	32	41	20	7
June 1977	29	41	23	7
Jan. 1978	30	42	21	7
June 1978	24	40	27	8
Nov. 1978	23	41	28	8
Jan. 1979	24	42	27	6
June 1979	24	37	30	9
Nov. 1979	22	39	31	9
Mar. 1991	26	40	27	6
Dec. 1995	20	48	25	6

Source: Surveys by Roper Starch Worldwide, latest that of
December 1995.

TABLE 4–2
How Likely That You Will Lose Your Job? Selected
Years, 1975–1997
(percent)

Question: Thinking about the next twelve months, how
likely do you think it is that you will lose your job or be
laid off—is it very likely, fairly likely, not too likely, or not
at all likely?

	Poll	Likely	Unlikely
Jan. 1975	Gallup	15	81
Apr. 1975	Gallup	12	85
Oct. 1976	Gallup	12	85
1977	NORC	10	89
1978	NORC	7	93
Nov. 1979	Gallup	11	84
May 1980	Gallup	14	84
Sept. 1980	Gallup	15	84
1982	NORC	13	87
Jan. 1982	Gallup	15	82
May 1982	ABC/WP	23	75
June 1982	Gallup	15	81
June 1982	ABC	24	75
Aug. 1982	LAT	19	77
Nov. 1982	Gallup	19	77
Nov. 1982	LAT	19	79
1983	NORC	14	86
Apr. 1983	Gallup	16	81
Apr. 1983	LAT	16	83
Dec. 1984[a]	Black	23	73
1985	NORC	11	89
1986	NORC	11	90
Feb. 1987	ABC/Money	19	79
Oct. 1987	ABC	19	81
1988	NORC	9	91
1989	NORC	8	92
Feb. 1989	Gallup	12	88
Dec. 1989	LAT	12	82

(Table continues)

TABLE 4–2 (continued)

	Poll	*Likely*	*Unlikely*
1990	NORC	8	92
Mar. 1990	ABC/*Money*	16	82
July 1990	Gallup	12	86
Oct. 1990	Gallup	16	83
Dec. 1990	ABC/*Money*	13	86
1991	NORC	13	87
Mar. 1991	Gallup	12	87
June 1991	ABC/*WP*	19	80
July 1991	Gallup	15	84
Oct. 1991	ABC/*WP*	15	83
Oct. 1991	ABC/*WP*	18	81
Oct. 1991	Gallup	14	85
Nov. 1991	ABC/*Money*	19	81
Dec. 1991	ABC/*WP*	22	78
Feb. 1992	ABC/*WP*	19	80
Mar. 1992	ABC/*Money*	17	81
1993	NORC	12	88
June 1993	ABC/*Money*	21	78
June 1993	PSRA	15	83
Sept. 1993[a]	*LAT*	29	67
Dec. 1993	Gallup	12	86
1994	NORC	10	90
Oct. 1995[a]	*LAT*	30	68
1996	NORC	11	88
Mar. 1996	ABC/*WP*	22	76
Apr. 1996	Gallup	14	85
Dec. 1996	*NYT*	13	85
May 1997	ABC/*Money*	13	86
June 1997	Gallup	9	89

NOTE: Responses combined. Question wording varies slightly.
a. Question asks how likely you *or someone in your household* will lose a job.
SOURCE: Surveys by the Gallup Organization, National Opinion Research Center, ABC News/*Washington Post*, the *Los Angeles Times*, Gordon Black, ABC News/*Money*, Princeton Survey Research Associates, and the *New York Times*.

TABLE 4–3
EARN ENOUGH MONEY? SELECTED YEARS, 1992–1997
(percent)

Question: Do you now earn enough money to lead the kind of life you want, or not?

	Yes, Enough Money	No
Jan. 1992	39	61
May 1992	34	65
Aug. 1992	33	66
Oct. 1992	36	63
Mar. 1994	44	56
Feb. 1995	41	58
June 1996	44	56
Sept. 1996[a]	44	55
May 1997	46	54
Nov. 1997	41	59

To those who answered "no" to the above question, do you think you will be able to earn enough money in the future to lead the kind of life you want, or not?

Jan. 1992	34	22
May 1992	34	28
Aug. 1992	36	25
Oct. 1992	35	23
Mar. 1994	33	20
Feb. 1995	35	20
June 1996	34	20
Sept. 1996[a]	33	18
May 1997	34	18
Nov. 1997	33	24

NOTE: All respondents were currently employed.
a. Registered voters.
SOURCE: Surveys by Princeton Survey Research Associates for *U.S. News & World Report* (Jan. 1992–Oct. 1992); Times Mirror–Center for the People & the Press (Mar. 1994–Feb. 1995); and Pew Research Center for the People & the Press (June 1996–Nov. 1997).

TABLE 4–4
THE MIDDLE CLASS TODAY, 1994
(percent)

Question: Thinking now about how things are going in the country these days. . . . Do you think things are becoming better for the middle class, becoming worse, or are staying about the same?

	Better	Worse	Same
1994	8	57	34

Question: For each one, tell me whether you strongly agree, somewhat agree, somewhat disagree, or strongly disagree. . . . It's the middle class now, not the poor, who really get a raw deal today.

	Strongly Agree	Somewhat Agree	Somewhat Disagree	Strongly Disagree
1994	50	25	14	9

SOURCE: For top panel, survey by Yankelovich Partners, September 1994. For bottom panel, survey by Greenberg Research for the Democratic Leadership Council, November 1994.

TABLE 4–5
DO HIGH-INCOME FAMILIES PAY TOO MUCH IN TAXES?,
SELECTED YEARS, 1977–1992
(percent)

Question: For each one would you tell me whether you think they have to pay too much in taxes, or too little in taxes or about the right amount? . . . High-income families?

	Too Much	Too Little	About Right
May 1977	8	75	10
May 1978	7	76	9
July 1978	8	76	9
May 1979	8	75	9
Jan. 1985	5	80	10
Apr. 1986	7	77	10
Jan. 1992	9	72	10

SOURCE: Surveys by Roper Starch Worldwide, latest that of January 1992.

TABLE 4–6
DOES THE TAX SYSTEM BENEFIT THE RICH? SELECTED
YEARS, 1972–1995
(percent)

Question: I want to read off to you a number of things some people have told us they have felt from time to time. Do you tend to feel . . . the tax laws are written to help the rich and not the average man, or not?

	Help the Rich	Do Not Help the Rich
1972	68	25
1973	74	21
1974	75	19
1978	74	18

Question: I am going to read to you a few statements and I'd like to know for each one whether this does or does not describe the way you feel . . . . The present tax system benefits the rich and is unfair to the ordinary working man or woman.

	Does Describe	Does Not Describe
1983	75	20
1985[a]	72	24
1995	74	21

a. Question wording varies slightly.
SOURCE: For top panel, surveys by Louis Harris and Associates, latest that of June 1978. For bottom panel, surveys by Yankelovich Partners (1983, 1995) and by ABC News/ *Washington Post* (1985).

TABLE 4–7
THE RICH GET RICHER AND THE POOR, POORER, SELECTED
YEARS, 1972–1996
(percent)

Question: Now I want to read you some things some people have told us they have felt from time to time. Do you feel or not feel. . . The rich get richer and the poor get poorer.

Year	Yes
1972	67
1977	77
1985	79
1990	82
1991	83
1992	83
1993	81
1994	78
1995	79
1996	76

Question: For each statement, please tell me whether you completely agree with it, mostly agree with it, mostly disagree with it or completely disagree with it. . . Today it's really true that the rich just get richer while the poor get poorer.

Year	Agree	Disagree
1987	74	22
1988	76	21
1989	78	19
1990	78	19
1991	80	18
1992[a]	79	20
1994	71	27

NOTE: In a May 1990 Gallup poll, people said that 21 percent of all Americans were rich and 33 percent poor.
a. Question was asked five times in 1992. The last point is used.
SOURCE: For top panel, surveys by Louis Harris and Associates, latest that of December 1996. For bottom panel, surveys by the Gallup Organization (1987–1989) and by Princeton Survey Research Associates (1990–1994).

TABLE 4–8
THE ELIMINATION OF POVERTY, SELECTED YEARS,
1937–1989
(percent)

Question: Do you think poverty will ever be done away
with in this country? (Gallup)
Do you think poverty in the United States is a problem
that will be finally solved, or do you think it will always
be a major problem for our society? (*LAT*)
Do you think . . . an end to poverty in America . . . will
happen in your lifetime or not? (Harris)

	Will Be Done Away with	Will Always Be a Major Problem
1937	13	83
1964	9	83
1967	7	89
1985	8	89
1987	14	82
1988	9	89
1989	6	92

SOURCE: Surveys by the Gallup Organization (1937–1967,
1989), *Los Angeles Times* (1985), and Louis Harris and
Associates (1987–1988).

TABLE 4–9
WELFARE VERSUS TAX BREAKS, 1992, 1993, AND 1995
(percent)

Question: Do you think the middle class is being squeezed more by welfare programs for the poor and unfair advantages for minorities or the cost of tax breaks for the rich and unfair advantages for big business?

	Welfare for the Poor / Advantages for Minorities	Tax Breaks for the Rich / Advantages for Big Business	Both[a]	Neither[a]
1992	23	60	10	3
1995	27	55	12	2

Question: What's a bigger problem for this country right now: rich people not paying their fair share of taxes, or people on welfare getting benefits they don't deserve?

	Undeserved Welfare Benefits	Rich Not Paying Taxes	Both Equally[a]	Neither[a]
Oct. 1992	30	28	32	6
June 1993	31	31	33	2
Jan. 1995	40	24	30	3
Oct. 1995	40	20	35	3

a. Volunteered response.
SOURCE: For top panel, surveys by NBC News/*Wall Street Journal*, latest that of September 1995. For bottom panel, surveys by the *Los Angeles Times*, latest that of October 1995.

TABLE 4–10
DIFFERENCES BETWEEN HAVES AND HAVE-NOTS, SELECTED
YEARS, 1974–1995
(percent)

Question: Now here is a list of a number of different things that people have said may be happening in our society in the coming years. Would you read down that list and call off all those you think are likely to happen in the coming years? Would you read down that list again and tell me which ones you see as serious threats to our society and life as we know it in the United States? . . . Increasing the differences between the haves and the have-nots.

	Likely to Happen	Serious Threat to Society
1974	36	14
1976	36	14
1978	35	13
1980	39	15
1984	40	16

Question: I am going to read to you a list of things people have said may pose a threat to the future of the American Dream. As I read each one please tell me if you feel it severely threatens the future of the American Dream, somewhat threatens it, or doesn't threaten the future of the American Dream at all . . . A growing divide between rich and poor.

	Severely	Somewhat	Does Not
1995	38	44	14

NOTE: This point was ranked twelve out of twenty-two. It tied with "an emphasis by American business on the short term at the expense of the long term."
SOURCE: For top panel, surveys by Roper Starch Worldwide, latest that of March 1984. For bottom panel, survey by Roper Starch Worldwide, December 1995.

5
What Do We Want Government to Do about Inequality?

If the data on fairness are ambiguous, the data on what people want government to do about the gap between rich and poor are not. First, Americans do not want limits placed on how much people can earn.

In 1935, Elmo Roper, in his surveys for *Fortune* magazine, asked whether people believed "that the government should allow a man who has investments worth over a million dollars to keep them, subject only to present taxes?" At the time, Senator Huey Long was gaining national attention with his Share the Wealth campaign. Long proposed that no one be allowed to earn more than $1 million and that a floor of $2,500 would be provided for every person. In response to the Roper question, 45 percent said that government should allow a man who has investments over $1 million to keep them (46 percent disagreed). The categories Roper labeled as prosperous and upper middle class answered yes decisively; 40 percent of the lower middle class said yes, and 49 percent, no. Among those Roper labeled as poor, the percentages were 29 and 60 percent.

A grouping of similarly worded questions asked since 1939 finds not a single instance in which even 40 percent of those surveyed supported limiting people's incomes. The number favoring such a limit reached a high of 37 percent in a *Fortune* survey in April 1943, but it has usually been considerably lower (table 5–1). In 1993, the National Opinion Research Center asked whether people agreed or disagreed with the following statement: "People should be allowed to accumulate as much wealth as they can, even if some make millions while others live in poverty." Fifty-six percent agreed (11 percent strongly), 11 percent neither agreed nor disagreed, and 30 percent disagreed (6 percent strongly). Majorities of all income groups agreed with the statement, even those making less than $15,000 a year (table 5–2).

At the same time that people have "voted" against an income ceiling, they have consistently supported a wage floor. In 1936, 70 percent in a Gallup poll supported a constitutional amendment to provide for a minimum wage. Although an identical question was not asked when Congress debated a minimum wage hike in 1996, the overwhelming support for the increase (in most polls, 70 percent plus) suggests that support endures. At the same time, however, surveys show that people have strong reservations about government job guarantees.

Depending on how questions are worded, we get different impressions of public support for redistribution. But the data do not suggest a public clamoring for it. At one level, as shown in Gallup surveys conducted in 1984, 1987, 1990, and 1996, around six in ten said that money and wealth should be more evenly distributed (table 5–3). About three in ten felt that it was fairly distributed. But a question posed by Kluegel and Smith in their comprehensive inquiry about inequality seemed to support the status quo. A majority, 52 percent, thought that we should have about the present level of inequality. Thirty-eight percent said that there should be more equality of income, but only 3 percent wanted complete income equality (table 5–4).

In an international comparison, only 13 percent in the United States agreed with the statement that incomes should be made equal. A near majority was pulled in the direction of the statement "There should be greater incentives for individual effort" (see appendix). A different disposition about inequality exists in class-conscious Britain. In the BBC's May 1997 national exit poll, 57 percent of British voters agreed that the government should redistribute income from the better off to the less well off, while 15 percent disagreed.

Trend data in the United States show that support for government actions to redistribute income is not robust. In 1981, Princeton University political scientist Jennifer Hochschild wrote that "redistribution has been so far from the national consciousness that even voracious pollsters and doctoral students have, for the most part, ignored it."[15] "In the past 40 years," she said, "only eight questions on national surveys had investigated some aspect of redistribution of income. Only three of the eight mention wealth." Reviewing this meager collection of questions, Hochschild concluded that support for redistribution was strongest among the poor but that, even among this group, only a slight majority supported programs that would help them.

One of those early questions got directly to the point. In a 1939 survey for *Fortune*, Elmo Roper asked, "Do you think that our government should or should not redistribute wealth by heavy taxes on the rich?" Seventeen percent of those Roper called "prosperous" wanted this action, but 76 percent did not. The figures for the upper middle class were 28 percent and 64 percent. For those Roper described as "lower middle class," they were 34 and 57 percent. Among the poor, 46 percent wanted the government to redistribute wealth, and 40 percent did not.

In 1973, the National Opinion Research Center began asking people to think about government's responsibility in this area with this question: "Some people think that the government in Washington ought to reduce the income differences between the rich and the poor perhaps by raising the taxes of wealthy families or by giving income assistance to the poor. Others think that the government should not concern itself with reducing this income difference between the rich and the poor." NORC then gave people a card with a scale from 1 to 7, with point 1 meaning that the government ought to reduce income differences between the rich and the poor and point 7 meaning that the government should not concern itself with reducing income differences.

In 1973, 48 percent put themselves at points 1 and 2; 27 percent, at points 3, 4, and 5; and 22 percent, at points 6 and 7. By 1978, the next time the question was asked, the number placing themselves at points 1 and 2 was 30 percent; 49 percent were in the middle; and 20 percent were at points 7 and 8. In 1996, the figures were similar. In 1996, only 32 percent of those making less than $20,000 a year put themselves at points 1 and 2, supporting Hochschild's observation that even those in the lowest income groups were not especially enthusiastic (table 5–5).

Responding to a related but more direct question asked five times since 1985 by NORC, more people disagreed than agreed with the proposition that reducing the differences in income between people with high incomes and those with low incomes was a government responsibility. In the latest round in 1996, 42 percent disagreed, and 32 percent agreed. About a quarter put themselves in the middle, neither agreeing nor disagreeing. Thirty-eight percent of the lowest income group in the survey (those making less than $20,000 a year) agreed that this was a government responsibility, and 31 percent disagreed (table 5–6).

A survey taken in July 1997 by Penn, Schoen & Berland Associates, Inc., for the Democratic Leadership Council posed two questions about government redistribution. In response to the first one, 71 percent said that the role of the government was to "foster conditions that enable everyone to have a chance to make a high income," and 22 percent replied that its role was to "redistribute existing wealth." The second question asked people which of two statements was closer to their view. One-third chose "government should work to redistribute income to close the gap between the wealthy and the poor," and 64 percent selected "government should work to create opportunity, but not redistribute wealth." The American public is not sounding a call for government-directed redistribution.

TABLE 5–1
LIMITS ON INCOME, SELECTED YEARS, 1939–1994
(percent)

Question: Do you think there should be a law limiting the amount of money any individual is allowed to earn in a year?

	Yes	No
Feb. 1939	30	61
Dec. 1939	24	70
Mar. 1940	24	70
July 1942	32	60
Apr. 1943	37	52
June 1946	32	62
1980	21	79
Mar. 1981	20	75
Jan. 1992	9	83
Aug. 1994	22	74

Note: Question wording varied. Feb. 1939: Do you believe there should be a top limit of income and that anyone getting over that limit should be compelled to turn the excess back to the government as taxes? July 1942: Question begins "after the war." Apr. 1943: When the war is over, do you think it would be a good idea or a bad idea for us to have a top limit on the amount of money any one person can get in a year? June 1946: Do you think it would be a good thing for the country if the government put a top limit on the salary any man could make? 1980: Agree/disagree: There should be an upper limit on the amount of money any one person can make. Mar. 1981: Agree/disagree: There should be a top limit on incomes so that no one can earn more than $100,000 a year. Aug. 1994: Should there be a top limit on incomes so that no one can earn more than $1 million a year?
SOURCE: Surveys by Elmo Roper for *Fortune* (Feb. 1939–Apr. 1943); Opinion Research Corporation (June 1946); James Kluegel and Eliot Smith, *Beliefs about Inequality: Americans' Views of What Is and What Ought to Be* (1980 survey for 1986 book);Civic Services (Mar. 1981); Roper Starch Worldwide (Jan. 1992); and the Roper Center for Public Opinion Research/University of Connecticut for *Reader's Digest* (Aug. 1994).

TABLE 5–2
WEALTH ACCUMULATION, 1993
(percent)

Question: Please tell me whether you strongly agree, agree, neither agree nor disagree, disagree, or strongly disagree with . . . People should be allowed to accumulate as much wealth as they can even if some make millions while others live in poverty.

	Strongly Agree / Agree	Neither Agree nor Disagree	Disagree / Strongly Disagree
Total	56	11	30
Income			
<$15,000	51	12	33
$15,000–19,999	59	7	33
$20,000–29,999	54	11	34
$30,000–49,999	60	11	27
$50,000–74,999	60	10	27
>$75,000	65	12	22
Party			
Republican	66	10	22
Democrat	50	10	36
Independent	56	13	29

SOURCE: Survey by the National Opinion Research Center, 1993.

TABLE 5–3
FAIRNESS OF THE DISTRIBUTION OF MONEY AND WEALTH,
SELECTED YEARS, 1984–1996
(percent)

Question: Do you feel that the distribution of money and wealth in this country today is fair, or do you feel that the money and wealth in this country should be more evenly distributed among a larger percentage of the people?

	Distribution Is Fair	*Should Be More Evenly Distributed*
1984	31	60
1985	28	61
1987	27	66
1990	28	66
1996	33	62

Source: Surveys by the Gallup Organization (1984; 1987–1996) and the *Los Angeles Times* (1985).

TABLE 5–4
PREFERENCE FOR DEGREE OF EQUALITY IN SOCIETY, 1980
(percent)

Question: Some people say that incomes should be completely equal, with every family making roughly the same amount of money; others say that things should stay about the same as they are now; and still others think incomes should be less equal than they are now. Ideally do you think there should be . . . ?

Complete equality of income	3
More equality than there is now	38
About the present level of income equality	52
Less equality of incomes than there is now	7

SOURCE: Survey in 1980 by James Kluegel and Eliot Smith for *Beliefs about Inequality: Americans' Views of What Is and What Ought to Be*, 1986.

TABLE 5–5
SHOULD GOVERNMENT BE INVOLVED IN REDUCING INCOME
DIFFERENCES BETWEEN RICH AND POOR? SELECTED YEARS,
1973–1996
(percent)

Question: Some people think that the government in
Washington ought to reduce the income differences
between the rich and the poor, perhaps by raising the
taxes of wealthy families or by giving income assistance
to the poor. Others think that the government should not
concern itself with reducing this income difference
between the rich and the poor. Here is a card with a scale
from 1 to 7. Think of a score of 1 as meaning that the government ought to reduce the income differences between
the rich and poor, and a score of 7 meaning that the government should not concern itself with reducing income
differences. What score between 1 and 7 comes closest to
the way you feel?

	Government Should (points 1–2)	Midpoints (points 3–5)	Government Should Not (points 6–7)
1973	48	27	22
1978	30	49	20
1980	26	48	23
1983	31	44	22
1984	33	45	20
1986	32	49	18
1987	28	51	20
1988	29	50	19
1989	31	50	17
1990	33	48	16
1991	32	49	16
1993	29	49	20
1994	23	52	23
1996	28	50	20

(Table continues)

TABLE 5–5 (continued)

Government Ought to Reduce Income Differences
(points 1–2)

	1978	1984	1994	1996
Income				
<$20,000	32	35	27	32
$20,000–29,999	8	25	24	28
$30,000–49,999	6	19	16	20
$50,000+	28	27	20	20
Education				
<H.S. grad.	33	42	37	38
H.S. grad.	31	33	23	26
Some college	17	27	22	29
College grad.	21	19	16	21
Gender				
Male	28	31	19	26
Female	33	34	27	29

Government Should Not Concern Itself with Reducing
Income Differences (points 6–7)

	1978	1984	1994	1996
Income				
<$20,000	26	21	17	12
$20,000–29,999	42	23	26	20
$30,000–49,999	39	38	28	22
$50,000+	15	22	30	34
Education				
<H.S. grad.	11	10	17	13
H.S. grad.	17	21	21	18
Some college	28	23	25	21
College grad.	30	28	32	28
Gender				
Male	25	25	28	25
Female	13	16	20	17

SOURCE: Surveys by the National Opinion Research Center, latest that of 1996.

TABLE 5–6
GOVERNMENT RESPONSIBILITY IN REDUCING INCOME
DIFFERENCES, SELECTED YEARS, 1985–1996
(percent)

Question: What is your opinion of the following statement? It is the responsibility of the government to reduce the differences in income between people with high incomes and those with low incomes.

	Agree/Agree Strongly	Neither Agree nor Disagree	Disagree/Disagree Strongly
1985	30	20	50
1990	33	27	39
1993	31	21	46
1994	27	18	51
1996	32	24	42

Subgroup	Agree/Agree Strongly	Neither Agree nor Disagree	Disagree/Disagree Strongly
Income			
<$20,000	38	29	31
$20,000–29,999	34	20	44
$30,000–49,999	25	26	49
$50,000+	22	21	55
Education			
<H.S. grad.	35	26	31
H.S. grad.	33	24	38
Some college	32	23	43
College grad.	24	22	54
Postgraduate	29	23	48
Gender			
Male	29	22	47
Female	34	25	37

NOTE: All subgroup data taken from 1996 survey.
SOURCE: Surveys by the National Opinion Research Center, latest that of 1996.

6

Concluding Observations

Both authors of this study review polls daily and feel confident about the general impressions they yield. In many areas, the constancy of opinion is nothing short of astonishing. For sixty years, large majorities of Americans have rejected a government-imposed income ceiling. Just as decisively and for just as long, they have supported a wage floor for those who are working. But there are many gray areas. The poll picture of the American dream is muddled because the public's idiosyncratic individual judgments do not yield a clear collective judgment. On another issue important to this discussion, poll data simply are not adequate to tell us whether people believe that our system is less fair than in the past.

To reiterate our major points, Americans are ambivalent about, but not hostile to, wealth. In the face of a media bombardment of stories about fabulous salaries and extravagant lifestyles, people's own desires seem modest. We are a vast middle class reasonably satisfied with what we have and aware that many things in life are more important than money. We believe that individual efforts and talents go a long way toward explaining what we and others in the society have.

No society gives all its citizens the same chance to achieve all positions. But most Americans believe that their society provides opportunity to advance for those who are willing to work hard. This conviction does not appear to have eroded significantly over the forty-five years for which we have data. The emphasis that our country has historically placed on equality of opportunity and the strides that we as a nation have made where the ideal has not been fully realized—for African Americans and other minority groups and for women—sustain support for a standard of equal opportunity but not for a standard of equal outcomes.

Americans are not inclined to a politics of envy. They are inclined to the idea that opportunity is present to those who avail themselves of it. As a result, they are unsympathetic to government redistribution of wealth.

The free enterprise system functions best when it encourages accumulation and restraint. The latter quality seems noticeably absent in many areas of life today, a development that could make people more sensitive to economic inequality. Concerns about fairness are never far from the surface in our political life. If our vast middle class comes to believe that those at the top or bottom are gaining at their expense, that the odds are being rigged against those who work hard and play by the rules, the political importance of economic inequality will grow.

Appendix
International Comparisons

International Comparisons on Selected Issues Relating to Economic Inequality, Selected Years, 1990–1993
(percent)

	U.S.	U.K.	France	W. Germany	E. Germany	Japan	Hungary	Poland	Sweden	Australia
Equal opportunity to get ahead[a]	66	42	NA	55	25	41	18	27	NA	NA
Government-guaranteed minimum standard[b]	27	50	NA	57	80	61	81	55	NA	NA
Upper limit on income[c]	17	39	NA	32	60	36	58	47	NA	NA
Government provide jobs for all[d]	30	37	NA	46	84	66	80	66	NA	NA
Give equal shares[e]	19	30	NA	22	24	39	23	20	NA	NA
More wealth O.K. if equal opportunity[f]	43	23	NA	37	37	21	40	24	NA	NA
Incomes made more equal[g]	13	15	31	20	NA	14	NA	NA	13	NA

Individuals take more responsibility[h]	59	30	45	48	NA	11	NA	62	NA
Hard work brings better life[i]	59	38	37	43	NA	33	NA	34	NA
People can accumulate wealth only at other's expense[j]	13	15	13	12	NA	7	NA	13	NA
Can improve standard of living[k]	55	29	NA	34	39	NA	11	23	49
Law/medical students expect to earn a lot more[l]	70	71	NA	88	87	60	78	72	81
Large differences in income necessary[m]	26	19	NA	21	14	21	36	30	25
Inequality exists because[n]	58	65	NA	75	87	53	73	54	59
Income differences too large[o]	77	81	NA	84	98	84	86	60	63

(Table continues)

APPENDIX (continued)

	U.S.	U.K.	France	W. Germany	E. Germany	Japan	Hungary	Poland	Sweden	Australia
Government reduce income differences[p]										
	38	66	NA	66	89	NA	75	77	53	43
Government provide basic income[q]										
	35	68	NA	58	88	NA	85	87	46	51
Better income and standard of living than father[r]										
	58	72	NA	71	75	NA	51	47	NA	81
Better schooling and training than father[s]										
	74	68	NA	63	68	NA	64	59	NA	81
Government guaranteed job for all[t]										
	47	56	NA	66	93	NA	85	89	72	39

Key for survey organizations identified in the questions below:
ISJP = International Social Justice Survey. Data available from Inter-University Consortium for Political and Social Research, University of Michigan, Ann Arbor, Michigan. ISSP = International Social Survey Program. Data available from the Roper Center for Public Opinion Research, University of Connecticut, Storrs, Connecticut. WVS = World Values Survey. Data available from the Roper Center for Public Opinion Research, University of Connecticut, Storrs, Connecticut.

a. Percent responding "strongly agree" and "somewhat agree" to "Please tell me how much you agree or disagree with the following statement. In (country) people have equal opportunities to get ahead." Response categories were strongly agree, somewhat agree, neither agree nor disagree, somewhat disagree, strongly disagree (1991 ISJP).

b. Percent responding "strongly agree" to "Now I am going to read some statements that have been made about the role of the government in (country). Using one of the phrases on this card, please tell me how much you agree or disagree with each statement. The government should guarantee everyone a minimum standard of living." Response categories were strongly agree, somewhat agree, neither agree nor disagree, somewhat disagree, strongly disagree (1991 ISJP).

c. Percent responding "strongly agree" and "somewhat agree" to "The government should place an upper limit on the amount of money any one person can make." Response categories were strongly agree. somewhat agree, neither agree nor disagree, somewhat disagree, strongly disagree (1991 ISJP).

d. Percent responding "strongly agree" to "The Government should provide a job for everyone who wants one." Response categories were strongly agree, somewhat agree, neither agree nor disagree, somewhat disagree, strongly disagree (1991 ISJP).

e. Percent responding "strongly agree" and "somewhat agree" to "The fairest way of distributing wealth and income would be to give everyone equal shares." Response categories were strongly agree, somewhat agree, neither agree nor disagree, somewhat disagree, strongly disagree (1991 ISJP).

f. Percent responding "strongly agree" to "It's fair if people have more money or wealth, but only if there are equal opportunities." Response categories were strongly agree, somewhat agree, neither agree nor disagree, somewhat disagree, strongly disagree (1991 ISJP).

(Table continues)

121

APPENDIX (continued)

Now I'd like you to tell me your views on various issues. How would you place your views on this scale? One means you agree completely with the statement on the left, 10 means you agree completely with the statement on the right, or you can choose some number in between.

g. Percent responding within the 1–3 range to "Incomes should be made more equal" or "There should be greater incentives for individual effort" (WVS, 1990–1993).

h. Percent responding within the 1–3 range to "Individuals should take more responsibility for providing for themselves" or "The state should take more responsibility to ensure that everyone is provided for" (WVS, 1990–1993).

i. Percent responding within the 1–3 range to "In the long run, hard work usually brings a better life" or "Hard work doesn't generally bring success—it's more a matter of luck and connections" (WVS, 1990–1993).

j. Percent responding within the 1–3 range to "People can only accumulate wealth at the expense of others" or "Wealth can grow so there's enough for everyone" (WVS,1990–1993).

k. Percent responding "strongly agree" or "agree" to "The way things are in [country], people like me and my family have a good chance of improving our standard of living—do you agree or disagree?" Response categories were strongly agree, somewhat agree, neither agree nor disagree, somewhat disagree, strongly disagree, can't choose (1992 ISSP).

l. Percent responding "strongly agree" or "agree" to "Do you agree or disagree, no one would study for years to become a lawyer or a doctor unless they expected to earn a lot more than an ordinary worker." Response categories were strongly agree, somewhat agree, neither agree nor disagree, somewhat disagree, strongly disagree, can't choose (1992 ISSP).

m. Percent responding "strongly agree" or "agree" to "Do you agree or disagree, large differences in income are necessary for [country's] prosperity." Response categories were strongly agree, somewhat agree, neither agree nor disagree, somewhat disagree, strongly disagree, can't choose (1992 ISSP).

n. Percent responding "strongly agree" or "agree" to "Do you agree or disagree, inequality continues to exist because it benefits the rich and powerful." Response categories were strongly agree, somewhat agree, neither agree nor disagree, somewhat disagree, strongly disagree, can't choose (1992 ISSP).

o. Percent responding "strongly agree" or "agree" to "Do you agree or disagree, differences in income in (country) are too large." Response categories were strongly agree, somewhat agree, neither agree nor disagree, somewhat disagree, strongly disagree, can't choose (1992 ISSP).

p. Percent responding "strongly agree" or "agree" to "Do you agree or disagree, it is the responsibility of the government to reduce the differences in income between people with high incomes and those with low incomes." Response categories were strongly agree, somewhat agree, neither agree nor disagree, somewhat disagree, strongly disagree, can't choose (1992 ISSP).

q. Percent responding "strongly agree" or "agree" to "Do you agree or disagree, the government should provide everyone with a guaranteed basic income." Response categories were strongly agree, somewhat agree, neither agree nor disagree, somewhat disagree, strongly disagree, can't choose (1992 ISSP).

r. Percent responding "strongly agree" or "agree" to "Please think of your present job (or your last one if you don't have one now) compared with your father when he was about your age, are you better or worse off in your income and standard of living generally?" Response categories were much better off, better off, about equal, worse off, much worse off, I never had a job, did not have a father (1992 ISSP).

s. Percent responding "strongly agree" or "agree" to "Please think of your present job (or your last one if you don't have one now) and compared with your father when he was about your age, are you better or worse off in your schooling and training?" Response categories were much better off, better off, about equal, worse off, much worse off, I never had a job, did not have a father (1992 ISSP).

t. Percent responding "strongly agree" or "agree" to "The government should provide a job for everyone who wants one." Response categories were strongly agree, somewhat agree, neither agree nor disagree, somewhat disagree, strongly disagree, can't choose (1992 ISSP).

Notes

1. "Inequality," *Economist*, November 5, 1994, p. 19.

2. "Income Gap Is Issue No. 1, Debaters Agree," *Washington Post*, December 7, 1995.

3. "Corporate Killers: The Hit Men," *Newsweek*, February 26, 1996, p. 44.

4. "Politics: The Next Step; Dole Opens Drive in New Hampshire with New Theme," *New York Times*, February 14, 1996, p. 1.

5. June 1995 press conference.

6. January 9, 1997, speech to the Council for Excellence in Government, Washington, D.C.

7. Gordon S. Wood, *The Radicalism of the American Revolution* (New York: Alfred A. Knopf, 1993), p. 347.

8. James R. Kluegel and Eliot R. Smith, *Beliefs about Inequality: Americans' Views of What Is and What Ought to Be* (New York: Aldine de Gruyter, 1986).

9. Oscar Handlin, "The Idea of Opportunity," *Public Opinion*, vol. 5, no. 3 (June/July 1982): 2.

10. William Safire, *Safire's Political Dictionary* (New York: Random House, 1978), p. 19.

11. This effort to look at key words is imperfect at best. We searched the Roper Center's poll archive for these words. Although it is the most comprehensive historical database available, it does not include all the survey questions ever asked.

12. James Davison Hunter, "A State of Disunion?" *Public Perspective*, February-March 1997, p. 35.

13. Four survey questions spanning more than fifty years suggest that what the public means by fair tax structure may be a considerably less progressive system than the one we have now. In 1941, Gallup asked a cross-section of Americans "how much a family, with a total income of $100,000 a year—that is,

125

$2,000 a week—should pay in personal income taxes next year?" The public set the tax rate at $10,000, or 10 percent.

The emphasis of the 1952 Gallup question was different: "Many wealthy persons in the U.S. now pay as high as 90 percent of their income in federal income taxes." When people were asked whether they would favor or oppose Congress passing a law "so the Federal government could not take more than 25 percent, or one-fourth, of any person's income in taxes, except in wartime," a near majority (47 percent) favored such a law, but 45 percent did not.

A 1986 Roper Starch Worldwide question began this way, "Different people pay different amounts of federal income tax depending on their personal and family circumstances. Consider four different families with a husband, a wife, and two children." People were then asked how much families with incomes of $25,000, $50,000, $100,000, and $200,000 pay in federal income taxes per year and how much these families should pay. The median response for what the highest-income group families ($200,000) should pay was $25,000, or 12.5 percent. Those surveyed thought these families paid $15,000, or 7.5 percent.

The 1995 Roper Center/*Reader's Digest* question was similar to the Roper Starch Worldwide question. When asked, "What is the highest percentage you think would be fair for a family making $200,000 a year to pay when you add all their taxes together?" the median response was 25 percent. There were no differences in the responses of income groups.

14. Guy Molyneux served as a consultant to the Preamble Center study.

15. Jennifer Hochschild, *What's Fair: Americans' Beliefs about Distributive Justice* (Cambridge: Harvard University Press, 1981).

About the Authors

EVERETT CARLL LADD is the director of the Institute for Social Inquiry at the University of Connecticut. He is also the executive director and president of the Roper Center for Public Opinion Research, a private, non-profit research facility affiliated with the University of Connecticut since 1977.

Mr. Ladd's principal research interests are American political thought, public opinion, and political parties. Among his ten books are *American Political Parties: Ideology in America; Transformations of the American Party System; Where Have All the Voters Gone?* and *The American Polity* (all published by W. W. Norton).

An AEI adjunct scholar, he is a contributor to the *Weekly Standard*, a member of the editorial boards of four magazines, and the editor of the Roper Center's magazine, *Public Perspective*. In recent years, he has been a fellow of the Ford, Guggenheim, and Rockefeller Foundations; the Center for International Studies at Harvard; the Hoover Institution at Stanford; and the Center for Advanced Study in the Behavioral Sciences.

KARLYN H. BOWMAN is a resident fellow at the American Enterprise Institute. She joined AEI in 1979 and was managing editor of *Public Opinion* until

1990. From 1990 to 1995 she was the editor of *The American Enterprise*. Ms. Bowman continues as editor of the magazine's "Opinion Pulse" section, and she writes about public opinion and demographics. Her most recent publications include *Public Opinion in America and Japan* (with Everett Carll Ladd, AEI Press, 1996); "Public Attitudes toward the People's Republic of China," in *Beyond MFN: Trade with China and American Interests* (AEI Press, 1994); "Public Opinion toward Congress" (with Everett Carll Ladd), in *Congress, the Press, and the Public* (AEI-Brookings, 1994); and *The 1993–1994 Debate on Health Care Reform: Did the Polls Mislead the Policy Makers?* (AEI Press, 1994).

AEI STUDIES ON UNDERSTANDING
ECONOMIC INEQUALITY
Marvin H. Kosters, series editor

ATTITUDES TOWARD ECONOMIC INEQUALITY
Everett Carll Ladd and Karlyn H. Bowman

COMPARING POVERTY: THE UNITED STATES AND OTHER
INDUSTRIAL NATIONS
McKinley L. Blackburn

THE DISTRIBUTION OF WEALTH: INCREASING INEQUALITY?
John C. Weicher

EARNINGS INEQUALITY: THE INFLUENCE OF CHANGING
OPPORTUNITIES AND CHOICES
Robert H. Haveman

INCOME MOBILITY AND THE MIDDLE CLASS
*Richard V. Burkhauser, Amy D. Crews,
Mary C. Daly, and Stephen P. Jenkins*

INCOME REDISTRIBUTION AND THE REALIGNMENT
OF AMERICAN POLITICS
*Nolan M. McCarty, Keith T. Poole,
and Howard Rosenthal*

RELATIVE WAGE TRENDS, WOMEN'S WORK, AND FAMILY
INCOME
Chinhui Juhn

THE THIRD INDUSTRIAL REVOLUTION: TECHNOLOGY,
PRODUCTIVITY, AND INCOME INEQUALITY
Jeremy Greenwood

WAGE INEQUALITY: INTERNATIONAL COMPARISONS
OF ITS SOURCES
Francine D. Blau and Lawrence M. Kahn